2⁰⁰
ƙ

Surviving Salvation

The Ethiopian Jewish Family
in Transition

Dr. Ruth Westheimer
Dr. Steven Kaplan

NEW YORK UNIVERSITY PRESS
New York and London

NEW YORK UNIVERSITY PRESS
New York and London

Library of Congress Cataloging-in-Publication Data
Westheimer, Ruth K. (Ruth Karola), 1928-
Surviving salvation : the Ethiopian Jewish family in transition /
Ruth Westheimer, Steven Kaplan.
p.   cm.
Includes bibliographical references and index.
ISBN 0-8147-9253-7
1. Falashas—Israel—Social conditions.   2. Immigrants—Israel—
Social conditions.   3. Jewish families—Israel.   4. Israel—Ethnic
relations.   I. Kaplan, Steven. II. Title.
DS113.8.F34W47   1993
305.8'0095694—dc20   92-31753
CIP

New York University Press books are printed on acid-free paper,
and their binding materials are chosen for strength and durability.

Manufactured in the United States of America

c 10 9 8 7 6 5 4 3 2 1

Book design by Ken Venezio

I dedicate this book to my beloved parents and grandparents, who, in an indescribable sacrifice, sent me, their only child and grandchild, to safety and who perished in concentration camps.

The set of values, the joie de vivre, and the positive outlook they instilled in me live on in my life and the new family I have created to carry on their traditions.

And to my first grandchild, Ari Chaim Einleger.

R. W.

To my mother, Ruth Kaplan

S.K.

Leave your country, your kin and your father's house and go to the land that I will show you.

GENESIS 12:1

Contents

Illustrations

Acknowledgments

In order not to add another chapter, I will just mention the names of a few family members, friends, and colleagues who were instrumental in helping and in donating funds for the documentary film and their encouragement that led to this book: Fred Westheimer, Joel Westheimer, Miriam Westheimer-Einleger, Joel Einleger, Malcolm Clarke, Maria Cuadrado, Shlomo Josh Gafni, Floyd Haar, M.D., Rick Hodes, M.D. (American Jewish Joint Distribution Committee), Fred Howard, Mitchell Koss, Pierre Lehu, Louis Lieberman, Ph.D., Sandra Medof, Ambassador Asher Naim, Fred Rosenberg, Uri Savir, Amir Shaviv (American Jewish Joint Distribution Committee), Robert Stewart, Niko Pfund, our superb editor, Colin Jones, Director of New York University Press who makes decisions on the spot, and Despina Papazoglou Gimbel, Managing Editor, for her care with this book.

R.W.

Ellen Goldberg, Director of Amishav for JDC Israel, assisted in every stage of this project, from the original "shiduch" to the completion of the manuscript. In between she facilitated overseas communication, offered a detailed critique of the manuscript at various stages, and gave generously of her time and understanding. She is for both of us a cherished friend and valued associate.

Chaim Rosen commented generously on the manuscript and shared his unique insights concerning the Beta Israel in countless discussions.

Others who have commented on all or part of the manuscript include Hagar Salomon, David Satran, Shalva Weil, Belaynish Zevadiah, Danielle Conhaim, and Lisa Anteby.

Leora Peretz and Sharon Mussen provided access to material gathered in interviews they conducted in Israel in 1991.

Norma Schneider, always the complete professional, helped us to see the obvious and made it possible for us to publish this book with New York University Press.

The Harry S. Truman Research Institute of the Hebrew University provided research and office facilities.

Booshun and Yona Kaplan displayed enthusiasm, patience, and humor and made sure that their father kept his "celebrity" status in perspective.

S.K.

Surviving Salvation

Introduction

Anyone who has ever flown with the Israeli national airlines, El Al, knows it is an experience unlike that found on other airlines anywhere else in the world. From the minute the seatbelt sign goes off at the beginning of the flight until it is turned on again at the end, the entire plane seems to be in perpetual motion. Orthodox Jews, having somehow reckoned the appropriate time for the afternoon service while zooming across time zones, recite their prayers. Other passengers wander up and down the aisles, periodically discovering long-lost friends or just engaging in a quick round of "Jewish geography" with a new acquaintance. One meal has no sooner ended than the next one begins.

Yet even by the unusual standards of El Al, the Boeing 747 that made its way from the besieged Ethiopian capital of Addis Ababa to Ben Gurion Airport near Tel Aviv on May 25, 1991 was an extraordinary sight. For one thing it carried almost eleven hundred passengers, a record for civil aviation. They had boarded the plane in just thirty-seven minutes. Since the conventional flight safety announcements were rendered irrelevant by the crowding, they were omitted. Women were requested, however, to remove infants from their backcarriers during takeoff. Despite the inevitable discomfort of many of the passengers, the plane, which carried among its three hundred children a baby born only minutes before takeoff, was almost silent.

1.1.1. Initial pickup at Assade Maryam in the Gondar region. (Robert Lyons © 1991.)

Nor were the passengers particularly concerned with the in-flight meals (there were none), the fate of their luggage (even their carry-on was minimal), the in-flight movie (cartoons and El Al publicity films), or the possibility of long lines at customs or passport control. The hostess call buttons were quiet throughout the flight. Those who were familiar with the normal routine of international air travel, the crew, translators, and other staff on the plane, were far too involved with their history-making mission to give much attention to such mundane issues. The vast majority of the passengers, however, had never been on a plane or at an airport and had only one thought: After generations of longing and praying, they would soon be in the Promised Land. They were Ethiopian Jews, and "Operation Solomon" was bringing them to their new home.

The passengers on this one plane were less than 10 percent of the fourteen thousand Ethiopian Jews who arrived in Israel in less than thirty-six hours. Never had so many *olim* (immigrants)* entered the country in so short a period. The Jews of Ethiopia, who had waited longer than any other Jewish community to have their right to live in Israel recognized, were making up for lost time.

During the period 1980–1992, over forty thousand Ethiopian Jews left their native land and immigrated to Israel. Rarely in human history has an entire community been transplanted from one culture to another in such a short period. This book is about their experience in Israel. It is *not* about sex, and anyone looking for an updated version of Malinowski's classic *The Sexual Life of Savages* had better turn elsewhere. It is about families, and what happens to them under conditions of unusual change and stress. More specifically, it tells the story of the Beta Israel (Falasha)† of Ethiopia and how their families

---

* In order to keep the text as uncluttered as possible, we have provided only essential explanatory notes in the body of the book. A glossary of Amharic, Ge'ez (Ethiopic), and Hebrew terms and a selected bibliography appear at the end of the book.

†The issue of the "correct" name for the Jews of Ethiopia is a complicated one. Historically, they called themselves *(Beta) Israel* (The House of) Israel, but were most commonly referred to by others as *Falasha* (landless, wanderers). In Israel today, they are usually called *Yehuday Etiyopia* (Ethiopian Jews), and reject the name *Falasha* as derogatory. In the first chapter of this book, this shift in terminology will be shown to

have changed since they came to Israel. In it, we have tried to understand how a people whose physical salvation has been achieved struggle to insure their spiritual and cultural survival.

Per capita, Ethiopian Jews are undoubtedly one of the most written-about groups in the world. With a total population, including those born in Israel or still in Ethiopia, of a little over fifty thousand, they have been the subject of thousands of reports, articles, and even a fair number of books. Half a dozen volumes have been written, for example, about the rescue effort known as "Operation Moses." Three Hebrew books have analyzed their status under Jewish and Israeli law. A similar number of anthologies offer a sample of their religious texts. Yet, with the exception of a Dutch doctoral thesis compiled when less than eight thousand Ethiopians had reached Israel, no general study of their integration has been published.

The lack of a concise guide to this most recent chapter in Ethiopian Jewish history is certainly not due to a shortage of either interest or research. Countless popular articles have highlighted one or another facet of this story, and at one point no less than fifty scholars claimed to be engaged in research on the group. Paradoxically, therefore, while the Ethiopians are among the most studied of all immigrants to Israel, most people have found it difficult to learn about them. Through this small book, we hope to offer a partial remedy to this problem. It offers an overview of Ethiopian life in Israel that we hope will serve as a useful introduction to the subject.

In this book we have focused on the crucial issue of family life as the key to understanding the Ethiopians' experience in Israel. We have chosen this subject for a number of reasons. On the most immediate level, it is the obvious subject for these two authors, one trained in the interdisciplinary study of the family, the other in Ethiopian history and culture. Moreover, the changes undergone by Ethiopian families in Israel—as couples divorce and remarry, children assert an unprec-

---

be an important marker of larger cultural changes. We will of necessity use all three terms: Beta Israel, Falasha, and Ethiopian Jews. Throughout the remainder of the book, the last of these terms will be used almost exclusively.

2.I.2. Ethiopians in Israel demonstrating for family reunification, 1984.
(Doron Bachar, Beth Hatefutsoth.)

edented degree of independence and women redefine their roles—lie at the heart of the Ethiopian experience in Israel. Almost everyone who has met or worked with Beta Israel immigrants has commented on the upheavals they have weathered in their domestic lives.

The changes we are considering, however, are by no means limited to the internal turmoil just mentioned. The Ethiopians' move to Israel has not only redefined roles within their families but has also radically changed the families' relationship with the surrounding society. In Ethiopia, the Beta Israel were united by a shared faith and a broad network of kinship ties. Families and households were the foundation of rural communal society and played a far greater role in the life of the individual than they do in most industrial societies. Families served as schools, workshops, clinics, reformatories, and credit organizations. In Israel most of these functions have become the primary responsibility of other institutions. Families, having been forced to give up many duties, must adjust themselves to their new position in the wider community.

Therefore, no understanding of the Beta Israel in Israel would be complete without a discussion of their families and the changes they have undergone. Our focus on the family, moreover, far from limiting us to an aspect of the Ethiopian experience that has few parallels in Israel or elsewhere, allows us to reveal the universality of their experience. The transformation of families under new conditions is, for example, one of the key themes of all *aliyot* (immigrations to Israel), of virtually all movements of refugees and immigrants anywhere in the world, and of the worldwide transition from preindustrial to industrial societies. While neither of us has experienced the last of these processes personally, both have immediate experience of the other two. It is, therefore, with special interest that we turn to this subject.

Although this book is about the evolution of Ethiopian family life in Israel, the changes they have undergone since *aliyah* can only be properly understood within the framework of their history in twentieth-century Ethiopia. We have begun our book, therefore, with a survey of events during this period, which culminated in the dramatic airlifts that brought many of the Beta Israel to Israel. We next turn our attention to a general discussion of their resettlement in Israel and the challenges they face. Particular attention is given to the interaction between the Ethiopians and such Israeli institutions as the Chief Rabbinate, the Jewish Agency, and the Ministry of Immigrant Absorption. The succeeding three chapters, which form the heart of this book, offer detailed analyses of parent-child relations, changes in gender roles, and marital relations. In each of these chapters, we compare life in Ethiopia with that in Israel and try to understand the nature of their changes and their implications. In the final chapter we consider some of the innovative programs that have been designed to assist the Ethiopians in their efforts to survive as a healthy, dynamic people in their new homes.

This book could not have been written without the help of all those we have mentioned in the acknowledgments. More significantly, the story it seeks to tell would not have come about were it not for the courage, daring, imagination, and dedication of countless individuals and organizations. Inevitably, in the course of their activities, there were errors both of judgment and of execution. We do not intend to ignore these. Neither, however, have we set out to write an exposé. Rather, we seek to understand the combined efforts of both immigrants and those assisting them to build a shared future.

This book is the product of as unlikely a pairing of authors as one is likely to encounter, and many readers are probably curious as to how the world's most famous psychosexual therapist teamed up with a scholar whose previous works included a study of medieval Ethiopian monks. Like many people, Dr. Ruth was captivated and moved by the dramatic scenes broadcast around the world at the time of Operation Solomon. For her, however, as a Holocaust survivor who had immigrated to Israel as a 17-year-old orphan, they struck a deeper chord than for most. Almost immediately, she began to make plans for a documentary film that would tell the story of these latest immigrants and those who had preceded them. Working with her usual energy and speed (which is something like a hurricane at fast-forward), she had everything in place by July and was ready to start work in Israel.

In addition to assembling a film crew that included an Academy Award-winning director, and Emmy Award-winning producers, Dr. Ruth had also made contact with the Jewish Agency and the Joint Distribution Committee (JDC), two of the key organizations working with Ethiopian Jews in Ethiopia and Israel. Working closely with the JDC's director of special operations, Amir Shaviv, and its director in Israel of programs for Ethiopian immigrants, Ellen Goldberg, Ruth began to compile a list of topics to be explored and people to be interviewed. Among the latter was Steven Kaplan of Hebrew University, who had just completed a book on the history of Ethiopian Jews for New York University Press.

After hearing about each other for several weeks, we finally met over dinner with Ellen Goldberg's family in Jerusalem. Although only a quick exchange of ideas was possible, it soon became clear that there was much to discuss. We arranged to have lunch later in the week.

As she has done so often in the past, Ruth decided to forgo the normal formalities and trust her instincts. On the walk from the Laromme Hotel to lunch at the Jerusalem YMCA, before discussion of the film could even begin, she proposed collaboration on a book. Steve, in preparation for talking about the documentary, had brought with him two pictures of an Ethiopian family taken just before and just after their registration at an absorption center. These pictures, which appear on the cover of this book, concisely illustrate the speed with which changes have taken place in Israel. Worth the proverbial thousand (or in this case two thousand) words, they immediately provided a theme and focus for the book. Moreover, they also made it clear that there was a brilliant photographer, the Diaspora Museum's Doron Bachar, with a similar vision of the story. Less than an hour later, Doron was contacted in Tel Aviv. Most of the photographs in this book that illustrate Ethiopian life in Israel are his work.

However unusual the joint effort that produced this book may appear at first glance, it is on many levels quite appropriate. As was noted above, the disciplinary interests we bring to this book (the study of the family and Ethiopian culture) are precisely the combination it needs. Moreover, it neatly suits our professional goals. For

3.I.3. First day in Israel, Ashqelon. (Doron Bachar, Beth Hatefut-soth.)

4.I.4. Ethiopian immigrant girl in Israel. (Bruce Bennett.)

Ruth it offers the opportunity to remind people that she doesn't only talk about *sex*; for Steve, it offers the chance to share his ideas with a much wider audience than ever before.

Finally and most seriously, in turning to a story of flight, rescue, *aliyah,* and resettlement, we are both examining themes from our personal family histories. In 1939, the same year that the ten-year-old Karola Ruth Siegel left Germany en route to her refuge in Switzerland, Steve's mother (also Ruth) fled as a twelve-year-old from Germany to America. While Dr. Ruth's personal journey eventually led her to Israel and from there to America, Steve was born in the United States but eventually settled in Israel. Thus, we both bring to this book a keen sense that however unique the saga of the Ethiopian *aliyah* may be, it also contains many elements of wider Jewish and human significance. It is our hope that by the end of this book the reader will have come to appreciate this dramatic and moving story as much as we have.

CHAPTER ONE

From Falasha to Ethiopian Jews

The Falasha of Ethiopia

Virtually every book about the Jews of Ethiopia begins with a discussion of their history and in particular the riddle of their origins. In most cases the Ten Lost Tribes, King Solomon, and the Queen of Sheba figure prominently. One can scarcely blame writers for the use of this opening gambit. The Solomon and Sheba legend, which in its Ethiopian version includes the Queen's sexual entrapment by the king, is a marvelous story, guaranteed to capture almost any reader.

While it would be tempting, therefore, for us to dwell on this episode at some length, we shall not permit it to detain us. The curious reader can consult Steve Kaplan's book on Beta Israel history where he discusses this story in detail. As he shows there, neither the Queen nor her royal seducer, nor the Lost Tribes have any historical connection to the Jews of Ethiopia. Even more importantly, these questions of ancient history are of little if any relevance for understanding the processes that concern us in this book. The integration of Ethiopian Jews into Israeli society today can scarcely be said to depend on the manner in which one explains their origins.

For our purposes it is enough to note that for hundreds of years there existed in Ethiopia a people who called themselves the Beta Israel (the House of Israel), but were called by their neighbors Falasha (landless, wanderers). They practiced a peculiarly non-Talmudic form of Judaism, which included devotion to the Orit (the Ge'ez—Ethiopic—version of the Bible), but lacked most post-Biblical observances such as Chanukah, Purim, *tallithoth* (prayer shawls), *kippoth* (skullcaps), *teffilin* (phylacteries), and Bar Mitzvah.

In traditional Ethiopia, where veneration of the Old Testament was so entrenched that the Christians viewed themselves as *Daqiqa Israel* (Children of Israel), the Beta Israel were notable not so much for their devotion to the Bible and its traditions as for their rejection of Christianity and its tenets. Thus, while their religious practice and belief had much in common with that of the dominant Christians (circumcision, abstinence from pork, and devotion to the Sabbath), both groups usually stressed their differences, particularly the Jews' rejection of the New Testament, Jesus, Mary, and the saints.

The Beta Israel were also notable for their deep concern with personal and communal purity. Thus women were segregated in huts at the edge of the village when menstruating or after childbirth. Contact with non-Beta Israel, especially the sharing of food, also required a week of isolation and purification. Ritual immersion was, in fact, so central a part of Beta Israel life that their villages were typically situated near streams and rivers, and their neighbors claimed they "smelled of water."

Like most non-Christians, the Beta Israel could not usually own land. Hence they were forced to live as tenant farmers and supplement their income by engaging in crafts such as weaving, pottery, and smithing. As potters and smiths the Beta Israel were identified with the seemingly magical transformation of matter through the use of fire. They came to be seen as sorcerers, as *buda* (possessors of the evil eye), needed for their skills, feared for their powers. While such ideas were scorned by many educated Ethiopians, well into the twentieth century Beta Israel were being blamed for random mishaps and illnesses that befell their neighbors.

Although they had once been ruled by their own "kings," this ended in the seventeenth century when the Beta Israel ruler of Semien province was defeated by the Ethiopian emperor Susenyos. From that time onward, no formal centralized institutions existed among the

5.1.1. Mother with picture of her daughter, who has emigrated to Israel. (Robert Lyons © 1991.)

Beta Israel. So, while it is still convenient to speak of an Ethiopian Jewish "community," what really existed were a large number of scattered communities loosely linked by economic, political, religious, and kinship ties. Since the Beta Israel were loath to bring their disputes before the ruling Christians, communal elders, including religious leaders and family heads, mediated disagreements.

In the best of all worlds and the simplest of all books, we could now move on quite naturally to describe the manner in which all this changed when they arrived in Israel. Indeed, most descriptions of Ethiopian immigrants follow this pattern and read something like a parody of the weight loss ads one reads in so many magazines.

Before	*After*
Before I made *aliyah* to Israel, my life was traditional, nothing had changed for two thousand years. I respected my elders, practiced an ancient religion, and lived in conditions I can only describe as primitive.	In only a few short weeks everything has changed! I've met people from all over the world. I've celebrated holidays I never dreamed of, experienced twentieth-century technology, and left my parents far behind.

The true story is, of course, much more complex. For almost a century and a half, the Beta Israel were exposed to outside influences that slowly altered their religious life, social norms, and self-image. While none of the changes from this period had as immediate and overwhelming an impact as emigration from Ethiopia and *aliyah* to Israel, they cannot be ignored. For one thing, it is only possible to faithfully report the effects of the move to Israel if we begin with an accurate picture of what existed before. Moreover, as we shall now demonstrate, Beta Israel history during the century prior to their move to Israel contains many fascinating hints as to the fate that awaited them. The nature of their families, the structure of their religion, their relations with outside Jews, and their view of themselves all changed significantly in the twentieth century. Long before they made *aliyah* the Beta Israel of Ethiopia were on the road to becoming the Ethiopian Jews of today.

The Challenge of Modernity

The modern history of the Beta Israel can be said to begin in 1859 with the establishment in their midst of a Protestant mission under the auspices of the London Society for Promoting Christianity amongst the Jews. The arrival of these missionaries, whose colleagues sought to convert Jews throughout the world, inaugurated the Beta Israel encounter with Western modernity. Ironically, it also marks the first time in their history that they shared an experience with Jews outside Ethiopia. The missionaries of the London Society were, thus, the first group to treat the Beta Israel as "Jews" in the universal sense. Certainly, it was the mission's activities more than anything else in the period before the twentieth century that created their awareness of the existence of a more universal form of Jewish identity and brought them to the attention of World Jewry.

In response to the missionary threat a number of prominent Jewish leaders began to lobby for aid to be sent to the Beta Israel. In 1867, Joseph Halévy went to Ethiopia as the emissary of the Jewish philanthropic organization known as L'Alliance Israélite Universelle. He returned with a glowing report, telling his audience, "I know you will find it hard to believe that they are Jews because of their black skin, but I have spoken to them and they are very intelligent. I think that proves they are Jews!" *

Despite Halévy's unequivocal confirmation of the Beta Israel's Jewishness, and his enthusiastic support for the establishment of institutions to assist them, no action was taken for almost forty years. When it came, moreover, it resulted less from a community consensus than from the initiative of a single individual.

---

* Most direct quotes in this book are either original translations (from Hebrew, French, Amharic) or excerpted from English interviews with native speakers of those languages. Although every attempt has been made to preserve the speakers' original wording, material has been edited both to eliminate errors of grammar and syntax, and to improve the flow of the narrative. Unless otherwise noted all emphases have been added.

Faitlovitch and His Impact

The arrival in Ethiopia of Halévy's pupil Jacques (Ya'acov) Faitlovitch in 1904 marks a turning point in the history of the Beta Israel. Faitlovitch, who dedicated his life to the cause of Ethiopian Jewry, was, more than any other single person, responsible for their entry into Jewish history and consciousness. Indeed, the amazing scenes of Ethiopian Jews arriving in Israel after being airlifted from the Sudan or Ethiopia can truly be said to be the final culmination of his dreams. The common thread that ran through all aspects of his program on their behalf was the attempt to bring them closer to other Jewish communities. To this end, he sought to raise their standards of education and created a Western-educated elite capable of interacting on a more or less equal basis with their foreign Jewish counterparts. He also promoted an image of Ethiopian Jewry that was both familiar and attractive to European and American Jewish audiences. Thus, he portrayed the Beta Israel as an alien Jewish element in a strange African environment. In his report to Baron Edmond de Rothschild following his first visit to Ethiopia, he wrote

> When I was in Africa among the Falasha surrounded by tribes of semisavages, I felt an inexpressible joy in recording their energy, their intelligence, the lofty moral qualities that distinguish them. We can be proud to count among our own these noble children of Ethiopia, who, with a no less legitimate pride, boast of tracing [themselves] back to our origins, worshipping our God, practicing our cult.

To this day the popular image of Ethiopian Jews is largely that created by Faitlovitch less than a century ago. Perhaps even more importantly, many of Faitlovitch's policies and the changes he initiated foreshadowed the more intensive encounter of the Beta Israel with World Jewry many years later.

One major focus of Faitlovitch's efforts, for example, was the attempt to reform Beta Israel religion to bring it closer to "normative" Judaism. Among the innovations he introduced were the lighting of Sabbath candles, the recitation of the first Hebrew prayers, the use of the Star of David, and the observance of new holidays such as Simhat Torah.

He was far less successful in convincing the Beta Israel to abandon their practice of isolating menstruating women. In fact, his attempts at reform led to a short-lived boycott organized by the community's religious leaders. In the end the practice survived throughout the century. Indeed, more than eighty years later, Qes* Manasse, the most senior Ethiopian religious leader in Israel, is still reluctant to forsake the custom and decries the failure of other Jews to separate their women.

Similarly prophetic was the personal experience of Gette Ermias, one of the two Beta Israel youths whom Faitlovitch brought to Europe in 1905. Given up for dead by his family, Gette returned home after three years to find that his fiancée had been married to another! While unique in its time, such situations were commonplace among Ethiopians in the 1980s and 1990s, when the difficulties of *aliyah* produced great uncertainty and divided many families. In many cases, moreover, it was not a fiancée who was given up for dead, but a husband or wife, who only after many years was discovered to be still alive.

Faitlovitch worked on behalf of Ethiopian Jewry until his death in 1955. Overall, he was far more successful in shaping the image of the Beta Israel than he was in changing their religious practice and social customs. His legacy was, however, continued by his students, most notably Taamrat Emmanuel and, in later years, Yona Bogale.

In the Shadow of Zionism and Revolution

During the years immediately following the establishment of the state of Israel, no attempt was made to bring the Beta Israel on *aliyah*. Lingering questions concerning their Jewishness, as well as social, medical, and political considerations, all convinced successive Israeli governments to defer any decisive action. At the same time, however, efforts were made to strengthen their ties to World Jewry and Israel.

---

*Unlike most Jews, the Beta Israel did not have rabbis, but priests, known as Qes (pl.qessotch).

6.1.2. Yona Bogale, an Ethiopian Jewish leader in Israel in 1984. On the mantel are pictures of Gette Ermias and Taamrat Emanuel, both also students of Dr. Ya'acov Faitlovitch. (Doron Bachar, Beth Hatefutsoth.)

From 1953 to 1958 representatives of the Jewish Agency's Department for Torah Education in the Diaspora were active in Ethiopia. A seminar was established in the city of Asmara. Initially it catered primarily to the priests and elders; later it came to serve principally as a teachers' training program for over thirty students. Two groups totaling twenty-seven Ethiopian youngsters were also brought to the Kfar Batya youth village in Israel to be trained as future teachers and leaders of their fellow Ethiopians. Although most returned to Ethiopia, some remained in Israel and became the first Ethiopian Jewish immigrants. The programs initiated during this period produced many changes in the Beta Israel. Eventually a network of schools was established throughout the Gondar region, which at its peak served hundreds of students.

As in the days of Faitlovitch, the impact of their efforts was not felt evenly among all sectors of the population. While a few villages declined to have any contact with outside Jewry, most welcomed it. Some communities, particularly those in peripheral regions, remained largely unaffected. Others, in or near villages in which schools were established, underwent a more dramatic transformation. Not surprisingly, youngsters tended to adapt more quickly then their elders, and in some cases generational tensions developed. High Priest Uri Ben Baruch's description of the Gondar region in 1973 could easily have been made fifteen years later as a description of Ethiopian life in Israel: "The young teachers want to lead the people, but the priest and the heads of the elders don't want to surrender their leadership. . . . Because the young teachers have access to the government, Falasha follow them, and only adults and the elderly continue to obey the priests of old."

Such intergenerational tensions were further exacerbated following the Ethiopian revolution of 1974. Young people exposed to secular education and political indoctrination rejected the ways of their elders as old-fashioned. Some girls, given access to schooling for the first time, refused to stay in menstrual huts. Others rejected their customary task of fetching water for their families. A few balked at marriage for fear it would limit their access to new opportunities or reduce their chances of leaving their villages. Contacts with non-Beta Israel

7.1.3. Two *qessotch* in Ethiopia. (Robert Lyons © 1991.)

increased significantly as young people joined political organizations, were conscripted into the security forces, or simply sought the professional and educational stimuli available in urban areas.

A *Tale of Three* Aliyot

While the significance of such changes should not be minimized, they pale in comparison to what happened from 1977 onward. At the beginning of 1977, only about 150 Ethiopian Jews had grudgingly been allowed to settle in Israel. Today, fifteen years later, their number has risen to over forty thousand! Although it took place over a relatively short period, the *aliyah* from Ethiopia was not a single event, but a series of waves each of which had it own special characteristics.

Recognition and the Tigrean Exodus. Although it was generally not realized at the time, 1973 was a crucial year in the history of the Beta Israel. For twenty-five years the state of Israel and World Jewry had dithered over the question of Ethiopian Jewry. On the one hand, Ethiopians were not allowed to come to Israel as immigrants. The Kfar Batya students, some of whom stayed in Israel for over six years, were, for example, never given citizenship. On the other hand, the hopes and dreams of Ethiopian Jews were repeatedly stimulated by contacts and initiatives from abroad. Thus schools were opened, closed, and reopened yet again. Jewish organizations and individuals would periodically "discover" the Falasha, call attention to them, and then lose interest until the next discoverer came along. Almost the only way for Beta Israel to enter Israel was to disguise themselves as Christians wishing to make pilgrimage to the Holy Land.

In early 1973 the Israeli Ministry of Immigrant Absorption, having undertaken a comprehensive review of the situation, prepared a report calling for the cessation of all connections with the Beta Israel. Noting their ties to Ethiopia and the doubts raised concerning their status as Jews, it concluded that the Beta Israel were best left to fend for themselves in Ethiopia. Before the report was released, however,

Ovadiah Yosef, the Sephardi chief rabbi, issued a religious ruling recognizing the Falasha as Jews. Citing rabbinic opinions from more than four hundred years earlier, he stated that they were descendants of the lost tribe of Dan.

Rabbi Yosef's pronouncement brought no clear change in the fortunes of Ethiopian Jewry. Indeed, the breaking off of diplomatic relations between Ethiopia and Israel in the wake of the Yom Kippur War, in October 1973, if anything increased their isolation. It did, however, remove most doubts concerning the Jewishness of the Beta Israel, and thus made it possible for Jews in Israel and the Diaspora to agitate on their behalf. A number of groups, most notably the American Association for Ethiopian Jewry (AAEJ), sought to place the Beta Israel on the agenda of World Jewry and the state of Israel. Slowly, their controversial and sometimes confrontational tactics bore fruit.

From 1977 onward, successive Israeli governments began to turn their attention to the issue of Ethiopian Jewry. In that year, 121 Ethiopian Jews were brought to Israel as part of an "arms for Jews" deal between the Israelis and the Ethiopians. Unfortunately, in February of 1978 Foreign Minister Moshe Dayan revealed the military side of the agreement, and an embarrassed Ethiopian government terminated the arrangement. It was not the last time that Israeli indiscretion was to endanger the Beta Israel.

Rather surprisingly, the first significant wave of Beta Israel to leave Ethiopia were not those who had had the most contact with foreign Jews and Israelis. Starting in 1980, Jews from the relatively isolated regions of Tigre and Walqayit began to journey to the Sudan and settle in refugee camps. Some were to wait there for as long as two or three years before being taken to Israel.

Despite their sojourn in these camps, on the whole these first immigrants fared better then those who were to come later. Their *aliyah,* although at times painfully slow, was spared major disasters or unnecessary publicity. In the main, their families survived intact with the loss of relatively few members. Thus, they were able to reconstitute themselves rather quickly upon their arrival in Israel. Even when the fact that they have been in the country the longest is taken into account, they seem to have adjusted better than any other group of Ethiopians.

Operation Moses and Its Aftermath. By the end of 1983, over four thousand Beta Israel, virtually the entire Jewish population of Tigre and Walqayit, had reached Israel. The Sudanese camps, however, far from emptying out, became home to an ever-increasing number of refugees. Most were fleeing yet another famine in war-torn Ethiopia. A small number, Beta Israel from the Gondar region, were driven not by the search for food but by their desire to reach Israel. On their way to the Sudan, they faced countless dangers. Ethiopian officials might arrest them, *shifta* (bandits) might rob and murder them, their "guides" might take their money and abandon them. In the words of one immigrant, "We didn't have enough water, enough food and we were afraid of robbers, of the Army. . . . Our traveling was usually at night to make it more difficult [for them to find us]."

Despite these obstacles, what had hitherto been a trickle of Jewish emigrants became a flood in 1984, and by the middle of the year close to ten thousand Ethiopian Jews had crossed the border into the Sudan. As the situation in the refugee camps deteriorated and the mortality rate rose, the Israel government decided to abandon its policy of gradual immigration in favor of a more ambitious policy. During a period of less than two months starting in mid-November 1984, more than sixty-five hundred Ethiopian Jews were airlifted to Israel in what became known as "Operation Moses." It was, at the time, the most dramatic and perhaps the most politically sensitive of Israel's many clandestine *aliyot.*

Almost from the start, Operation Moses was an open secret as hundreds of translators, social workers, doctors, and immigration officials struggled to accommodate the new arrivals. Although strict censorship was imposed in Israel, this did not prevent several foreign papers from carrying reports accredited to reporters outside Israel. The rather dubious decision to conduct a full-scale public fundraising campaign to finance a hazardous and allegedly clandestine operation made any true attempt at concealment a joke.

On January 3, 1985, representatives of the Jewish Agency, Foreign

8.1.4. This blind grandmother was led all the way from Ethiopia to the Sudan by her grandson. (Doron Bachar, Beth Hatefutsoth.)

Ministry, and Ministry of Immigrant Absorption, in an apparent attempt to divert media attention from the airlift and toward those Ethiopians already in Israel, gave a detailed briefing to the local and foreign press. On January 5, the Sudanese government suspended the airlift.

The untimely disruption of Operation Moses left several hundred Jews stranded in the Sudan. The American and Israeli governments immediately formulated plans to rescue them. In early March, Vice President George Bush visited the Sudan and reached an agreement on the subject with President Jaafar Numeiri. A few weeks later, a further 648 Beta Israel were removed from the Sudan in a CIA-sponsored airlift labeled "Operation Sheba" or "Operation Joshua."

Operation Moses and the events surrounding it had a major effect on Ethiopian family life. Between January 1984 and August 1985 approximately ten thousand Ethiopian immigrants arrived in Israel. In addition, as many as four thousand died on the way to or in the Sudan. As a result, almost every Ethiopian who reached Israel during this period had both lost family members and left others behind in Ethiopia. Scarcely a single family survived intact.

Refugee life in the Sudan had, moreover, produced more subtle strains and changes. Since a woman without a husband was vulnerable to rape and assault, a new type of marriage developed in the camps. In these "Sudanese marriages" a man and a woman would, regardless of other attachments, live together as a couple. Although often sanctioned by family members and community elders as an unavoidable expedient, such marriages usually proved short-lived and rarely survived after the couple reached Israel.

Many of the new arrivals had not only lost loved ones but had also been unable to properly bury and mourn them in the camps. Thus they carried with them a double measure of guilt, both for having survived and for having failed to fulfill their spiritual obligations. In some cases, complete funeral rituals were performed only years later, when conditions in Israel made this possible.

For many, moreover, loss and separation were accompanied by uncertainty, as the fate of at least one family member remained unclear. Wives waited for word from their husbands, children from

9.1.5. Two brothers reunited in Israel in November 1984. (Doron Bachar, Beth Hatefutsoth.)

their parents, brothers from their sisters. False reports of the death of husbands and wives were common. Both in Israel and in Ethiopia "surviving" spouses often established new families only to discover later that their original mate was still alive. In other cases, new households were set up simply in response to years of separation. Family reunification became the watchword of the Ethiopian community in Israel and the need to press for continued *aliyah* was the only issue on which a consensus existed.

Addis Ababa and Operation Solomon. During the period from August 1985 until the end of 1989, a further two thousand immigrants arrived from Ethiopia. The reestablishment of diplomatic relations between Ethiopia and Israel in the fall of 1989 opened the possibility of a renewal of the *aliyah* movement, this time on a legal basis. Although immigration from Ethiopia was limited at first, a small flow of *olim* was allowed to arrive. By the summer of 1990, over twenty thousand Ethiopian Jews (their numbers swollen by the return of converts, a high birthrate, and the identification of previously overlooked villages) had traveled to Addis Ababa in the hope of receiving exit visas. The conditions encountered by the migrants were extremely difficult. Malnutrition, inadequate housing, and disease all threatened the Beta Israel.

"When they first arrived in Addis Ababa, many of them had actually walked from Gondar. So, many had walked several hundred miles," explained Rick Hodes, the medical director of the Joint Distribution Committee's (JDC) clinic in Addis Ababa. "They were tired, they were thin, they were malnourished, and they were dying at [the rate of] more than forty people a month. . . . In response to the medical program the death rate plummeted . . . to only three in the month of April 1990."

Although the combined efforts of the Israeli embassy, Jewish Agency, JDC, and other organizations did much to alleviate the immediate threat to the refugees, some forms of damage were unavoidable. Thus, for example, traditional patterns of communal village life were destroyed as Jews settled in scattered groups throughout the urban sprawl of the Ethiopian capital. Families, customarily the ultimate

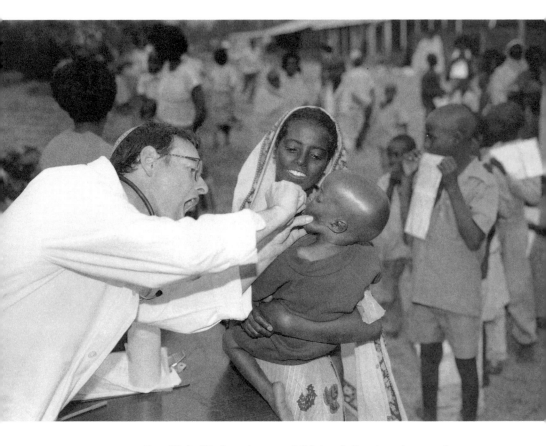

10.1.6. Dr. Rick Hodes gives a child its daily vitamin supplement.
(Robert Lyons © 1991, JDC.)

refuge and source of security in times of crises, found themselves completely incapable of providing for even their members' most basic needs. A 1991 report prepared by the Israel section of Defence for Children International noted that, faced with repeated examples of their parents' inability to cope with threats and dangers, many children lived "with a constant sense of insecurity . . . immersed in tension and anxiety."

Moreover, while the various agencies active in Addis Ababa saw to it that the basic needs of the refugees were met and thus avoided the catastrophic mortality rates associated with Operation Moses, the city held dangers of a new and different kind. Removed from their traditional occupational setting, many settled into a pattern of lethargy and dependence in which waiting for their monthly allowance from Israeli officials became a substitute for productive activity. Uprooted from the traditional norms of village life, many young people took advantage of the opportunity to sample the freedom and excitement of the city. Visits to prostitutes were common among young men removed from the control of their elders. Addis Ababa, like many African capitals, is unfortunately a hotbed for sexually transmitted diseases, including the HIV virus. Thus an unknown number were exposed to a fatal disease rarely found in their original rural surroundings.

The Beta Israel in Addis Ababa were, moreover, virtual hostages of Ethiopia's increasingly fragile Marxist regime. In exchange for their freedom the Ethiopian government sought political and military assistance from both Israel and the United States. In connection with these efforts the Ethiopian ruler Mengistu Haile Mariam paid a secret visit to Israel in the fall of 1990. As the result of intensive negotiations involving the United States as well as Ethiopia and Israel, it was finally agreed that between one thousand and fifteen hundred Beta Israel would be permitted to emigrate every month on the basis of family reunification.

Throughout the first months of 1991 the internal political situation in Ethiopia continued to deteriorate. Israeli negotiators led by Uri Lubrani sought to secure their rescue, while at the same time American officials, including President George Bush's special envoy, former senator Rudy Boschowitz, attempted to put together a deal that would both secure the safety of the Beta Israel and limit bloodshed. In the middle of May, President Mengistu fled to the Zimbabwean capital of Harare. As rebel forces approached the capital, fears grew that the Beta Israel would be trapped in what threatened to be a bitter struggle. Finally, only one obstacle remained to be overcome before they could be released: money. Almost overnight thirty-five million dollars were raised and paid to the Ethiopian government.

During thirty-six hours between May 24 and May 25, over fourteen thousand Beta Israel were airlifted to Israel in "Operation Solomon." Operation Solomon was by far the most diverse of the Ethiopian *aliyot*. In the past, the vast majority of Beta Israel who had reached Israel had been rural peasants, with little education or experience of modern conditions. Operation Solomon, while including a large number of Ethiopian Jews from some of the most isolated and underdeveloped regions in the country, also brought a fair number of educated city dwellers, some with professional training. This latter group of immigrants was largely made up of those who had not so much been "pulled" by the lure of Israel as "pushed" by the worsening conditions in Ethiopia.

On the most basic of levels, Operation Solomon was vastly successful in ending the problem of family reunification. With the *aliyah* of over 90 percent of all Beta Israel, only a relatively small number of family members remained in Ethiopia. (According to most reports, several thousand still remained in Ethiopia, as well as an undetermined number of *faras moura*, Christians of Beta Israel ancestry. Efforts began almost immediately to bring the former to Israel.) To be sure, it often took Ethiopians weeks and even months to actually locate relatives brought to Israel, but a clearing house was soon set up to make such searches easier. The end to this well-defined problem of physical separation served in many cases, however, to highlight a whole series of related issues. Husbands and wives separated for many years often found that their spouses had established new families in either Ethiopia or Israel. Those newly arrived in Israel frequently felt estranged from their *vatiqim* (old-timer) relatives. Those who had left their parents in Ethiopia when they were mere children were now teenagers or even young adults. In some cases, grandparents were shocked to encounter grandchildren unable to speak Amharic (although they generally understood it).

A New Beginning

Taken separately and individually the changes we have discussed in this chapter might not be considered of great significance. The Beta Israel, after all, still spoke the same language, ate the same food, and wore the same traditional clothes. The cumulative impact of events in the twentieth century was, however, tremendous. Long before the Beta Israel began to emigrate from Ethiopia, their religious and social life was in flux. External Jewish influences, coupled with processes of modernization originating in Ethiopia, had slowly but surely begun to transform their self-image and internal organization.

The manner in which most Ethiopians reached Israel further weakened the resilience of their families and community. Scarcely any Beta Israel immigrants moved directly from their villages to their new homes. Some, particularly the better educated, had lived for several years or longer in cities such as Addis Ababa and Gondar. This relatively small group was at least spared the destructive effects of long periods spent as displaced persons dependent on the charity of others. Many more languished in Sudanese refugee camps for months and even years. In 1990 and 1991 over twenty thousand lived for an extended period as illegal migrants in Addis Ababa and were supported by various organizations. In each case, those who arrived in Israel were months or even years removed from traditional village life. Many had grown accustomed to inactivity and living off charity. Scarcely a single family existed that had not experienced separation, divorce, death, and reorganization. Their arrival in Israel marked not the end of their struggle but its elevation to a new plane. Having achieved salvation, they now struggled to survive both as independent individuals and as a cultural group. It is this part of their story that we turn to in the rest of our book.

Strangers in the Promised Land

Israel's success record in secret operations under the harshest of conditions is unrivaled by that of any other country. Operation Solomon was only the latest in a long series of missions that included the kidnapping of Adolf Eichmann, the raid at Entebbe, the bombing of the Iraqi nuclear reactor, and, of course, Operation Moses. Unfortunately, perhaps, the resettlement of the Ethiopians is neither secret nor dramatic. It is, in fact, a long, complex process whose heroes usually go unnoticed.

At first glance, it appears rather strange that a country that is so good at carrying off the impossible struggles so much with the possible. One does not have to look far, however, to find the explanation for this apparent paradox. Rachamim Elazar, one of the leading spokesmen for Ethiopian Jewry, defines the problem succinctly: "Israelis love the dramatic. But whenever anything takes too long, politics takes over. This ministry fights that ministry; this party, that party. Everyone looks out for himself, and forgets the immigrants."

Elazar's words could easily apply to the Israeli handling of almost any issue. They have a special significance, though, when applied to the treatment of immigrants, and particularly the Ethiopians. Due to their constant reliance on the government and other helping agencies, Ethiopian immigrants are particularly vulnerable to the mistakes, oversights, and manipulations of others. Thus, even their most basic needs, such as education and housing are frequently entangled in disputes over jurisdiction, responsibility, and authority. During the period of Operation Moses, for example, the Ministry of Immigrant Absorption was controlled by the Labour party, while the Jewish Agency's immigration department was in the hands of the Likud. The Ethiopians were virtually the only immigrants arriving in the country, and each organization wanted them under its control. At times, the two bodies appeared so involved in political infighting that helping immigrants appeared to be only a minor side line. Few if any decisions were made regarding the Ethiopians that were not influenced by party political considerations. The involvement of other ministries such as Housing, Education, and Health only complicated the maneuvering.

There is a second, more profound cause for this confusion and muddle that reaches far beyond the realm of organized politics. The arrival of immigrants in Israel serves both to point out the issues that unite the country and to highlight those that divide it. Immigration, particularly of Jews in distress, lies at the heart of Israel's raison d'être. The treatment and integration of immigrants thus symbolizes the country's most cherished ideals. At no time was this clearer than during the arrival of the Ethiopians, which was greeted with an excitement that verged on euphoria.

Israel today, more than forty-four years after its founding, is, however, also a state in which many central issues of national identity remain unsettled. These controversies immediately rise to the surface when absorption programs are designed and implemented. Thus, the unique Ethiopian form of Judaism raises major questions as to the limits of religious pluralism in a Jewish state. Their distinctive cultural heritage highlights the perennial challenge of achieving social integration without cultural disintegration. Their inability to purchase housing on the open market forces policymakers to determine where, when, and in what numbers they should be resettled at different sites around the country. Their arrival as penniless refugees demands from those working with them on-the-spot decisions regarding the extent of government assistance and how best to wean them from it at a later date.

Every one of these issues directly impinges on our main theme, the

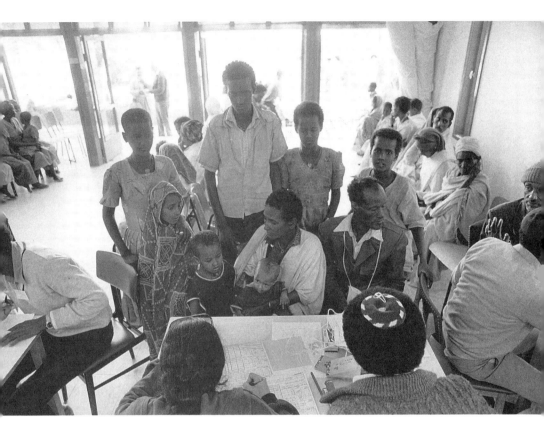

11.2.1. A family being registered in Ashqelon, 1984. (Doron Bachar, Beth Hatefutsoth.)

Ethiopian family. Each is, moreover, so complex as to require a separate discussion. In this chapter, we shall analyze four topics—religion, housing, dependency, and culture—that are contributing to the transformation of the Ethiopian family.

The Ethiopians and the Rabbis

Any description of Ethiopian life in Israel must begin with a discussion of their relationship with the country's religious authorities. No other issue reveals as clearly the manner in which their needs have become entangled with the controversies that divide Israeli society as a whole. No other topic has been the subject of as much controversy and confusion.

As noted in the previous chapter, Rabbi Ovadiah Yosef's decision to recognize the Jewishness of the "Falasha" was a turning point in their history. In fact, without this judgment in their favor, there quite probably would have been no Ethiopian *aliyah*.

Rabbi Yosef's pronouncement not only opened the doors to a more active policy in favor of Ethiopian immigration; it also placed those Ethiopian Jews who did arrive under the religious jurisdiction of the Chief Rabbinate. Since the time of the British mandate the Chief Rabbinate has been recognized as the supreme religious body of the Jewish community in the land of Israel. In particular, the Chief Rabbinate and the religious courts that it sanctions have exclusive jurisdiction over the matrimonial affairs of all Jewish residents. Jews may wed only in an Orthodox ceremony after the marriage has been registered with the Rabbinate. Only rabbis approved by the Chief Rabbinate may conduct weddings.

The Rabbinate's monopoly on religious services proved problematic for the Ethiopians. Although the Chief Rabbis had affirmed the *communal* status of the Ethiopians as Jews, they continued to express reservations concerning the *personal* status of individuals. In particular, they voiced their concern that the Ethiopians' ignorance of Rabbinic law (Halacha) had rendered divorces and conversions performed in Ethiopia invalid. According to the Rabbinate, non-Halachic conversions had resulted in hundreds of non-Jews immigrating from Ethiopia. Non-Halachic divorces had, they claimed, also raised considerable questions about the danger of *mamzerut* (illegitimacy) among the Ethiopians. (According to Jewish law a *mamzer* is the child of a couple whose sexual relationship is forbidden. In the case of the Ethiopians, the Rabbinate argued that invalid divorces had resulted in individuals still legally married remarrying and producing illegitimate offspring.)

In either case, grave difficulties existed with regard to a simple and immediate integration of the Ethiopians into the general Jewish population. Ethiopian immigrants strongly rejected both claims.

The Rabbinate attempted to resolve these doubts through a novel solution. Throughout the 1970s and early 1980s Ethiopian immigrants to Israel were required to undergo a modified conversion ceremony consisting of ritual immersion, a declaration accepting Rabbinic law, and (in the case of men) a symbolic recircumcision. Although initially applied to all Ethiopians, the requirement was eventually limited to those wishing to marry. Toward the end of 1984, the demand for recircumcision was dropped.

During the period from 1980 to 1984 several thousand Ethiopian immigrants, mainly from Tigre province, submitted to the demands of the Rabbinate. In many cases the precise nature of the ceremony performed was not explained to them; in some instances coercion was used. Nevertheless, prior to the middle of 1984, the vast majority of Ethiopian immigrants had agreed to normalize their religious status. From that period onward, however, organized resistance to the conversion ceremony became increasingly apparent. Recently arrived immigrants, acting on the advice of more experienced Ethiopians, refused to cooperate with the Rabbinate. Their resistance culminated in a month-long protest against the Rabbinate in the fall of 1985.

Those Ethiopians who refused to comply with the Rabbinate's demands found themselves in a bizarre situation. As Jews in Israel, they could only marry under the auspices of the Chief Rabbinate. As Ethiopians whose personal status was unsettled, they could not register to marry. Effectively, then, hundreds of them were denied the right to marry.

12.2.2. Qes Iyellin in dispute with a group of ultra-Orthodox Jews, 1984. (Doron Bachar, Beth Hatefutsoth.)

13.2.3. Ethiopians demonstrating against the Chief Rabbinate, September 1985. (Doron Bachar, Beth Hatefutsoth.)

In response to this anomalous situation and as a form of protest, some Ethiopians began to marry in traditional ceremonies conducted by their own religious leaders, the *qessotch*. Such marriages, although completely valid within Ethiopia, had no legal status in Israel and were not accepted by authorities. Couples wed in this manner could, however, by visiting a notary, gain recognition of theirs as a common-law marriage, which assured them of being treated as a couple for most purposes, including housing. The number of *"qes* marriages" dropped significantly following the appointment of Rabbi David Chelouche of Netanya, a prominent supporter of the Ethiopians, as marriage registrar for the entire community. Under this compromise, sanctioned by the Israeli Supreme Court, any Ethiopian in the country could travel to Rabbi Chelouche to register to be married.

While the appointment of Rabbi Chelouche provided a solution that preserved both the Ethiopians' dignity and the Rabbinate's sovereignty, bitterness over the dispute lingers. Many Ethiopians, for example, remain reluctant to undertake any act that might be misinterpreted as immersion for the purpose of conversion, such as visiting a ritual bath *(mikve)* or even swimming in a public pool. Others resent the fact that they alone among the Israeli population must make a journey to a single registrar in order to marry in the manner they prefer. Ethiopian political activists still speak with scorn and anguish about those who had been forced "to drop their pants" (surrender), a figurative reference to recircumcision and the deep humiliation and emasculation it implied.

Houses or Homes?

When viewed as a political-religious problem, the Ethiopians' conflict with the Rabbinate was scarcely typical of their dealings with most Israeli authorities. The Rabbinate's monopoly over religious affairs and its immunity to electoral pressure enabled it to weather the protest with equanimity. Far more characteristic of the Ethiopians' integration into Israeli society were their dealings with the various bodies involved in providing temporary and permanent housing. In

14.2.4. A typical Ethiopian *tukel* of the sort inhabited by many Beta Israel. (Robert Lyons © 1991.)

this case, philosophical differences, political considerations, bureaucratic infighting, and the Ethiopians' seemingly inexhaustible willingness to wait for the authorities to offer them what they demanded all played a role.

Of all the challenges facing the Israeli immigration authorities, none has proven more complex and fraught with difficulties than resettling the Ethiopians in permanent housing. Apartments, unlike language courses, job-training programs, health facilities, and many other services offered to new *olim* cannot be easily produced in response to a sudden rise in demand. If vacancies exist, they are usually in less desirable areas, which are the least equipped to deal with a large influx of newcomers. Settling too many immigrants in a single location can lead to their being ghettoized; settling too few can leave them isolated and makes it difficult for helping agencies to reach them. Housing decisions are among those with the broadest impact, for they affect educational opportunities, employment prospects, and social integration. Housing mistakes are also among the hardest to correct, for rebuilding is usually impractical, and repeated moves are almost always disruptive.

During the massive wave of *aliyah* from North Africa in the 1950s, most immigrants were housed in transitional camps known as *ma'a-barot*. Later many were resettled in "development towns," planned cities in sparsely populated peripheral areas. Although it was hoped that such towns would eventually flourish, development towns have largely remained underdevelopment towns, whose populations are among the economically and socially weakest in the country.

Long before the Ethiopians reached Israel, many of the shortcomings of earlier absorption policies had been recognized. This learning experience, coupled with a tremendous increase in the resources available, had led to numerous changes. Thus immigrants were channeled into "absorption centers" where their initial adjustment could be eased. During a period of several months their basic needs were cared for and they were taught Hebrew, familiarized with their new country, and, in the case of the Ethiopians, acquainted with the basic norms of Western culture and technology.

Ironically, although absorption centers offer immigrants many opportunities and benefits, they effectively deny the possibility of being absorbed into the surrounding society. As "total institutions" that exercise almost complete control over the lives of residents, they offer few occasions for interaction with the population outside the center. During the period immediately following Operation Moses, for example, most absorption centers were run as closed areas with no access to the general public. Even guests invited by the Ethiopians themselves had to be granted permission by the center staff to enter the facility.

For their part, the Ethiopians quickly grew accustomed to having outsiders meet all their needs. Indeed, for survivors of months or even years in refugee camps, living off charity came quite easily. Many were doubtless prepared to see their status as wards of the state prolonged indefinitely. They were, accordingly, shocked when their guardians began to withdraw services and attempted to relocate them into permanent housing.

The transfer of the Ethiopians out of the absorption centers proved immensely difficult. To begin with, no consensus existed at the time of Operation Moses as to how long they should stay in the centers. The Ministry of Immigrant Absorption, which had no responsibility for those in centers, argued that the Ethiopians' period in such a protected environment should be minimized to prevent them from becoming overly dependent on outside assistance. The Jewish Agency, which ran the centers, took the position that only extended long-term care could rehabilitate the traumatized victims of Sudanese refugee camps. Almost every time a group of Ethiopians was relocated, criticisms were heard about the timing, location, and method of the move.

While both bodies agreed that attempts should be made to avoid concentrating too many Ethiopians in a single region, city, neighborhood, or building, it was in practice almost impossible to achieve the desired degree of dispersion. Moreover, their plans often put them in open conflict with the Ethiopians, who wished to live as close as possible to family members. In general, the longer the Ethiopians were in the country, the more specific their housing preference became, and the harder it was to move them out of the centers.

15.2.5. A woman outside her apartment in Ma'aleh Adumim, 1986. (Doron Bachar, Beth Hatefutsoth.)

Anthropologist Chaim Rosen of the Ministry of Absorption describes one case:

> There was a group of Ethiopians put in an absorption center near Jerusalem, and a small group of them were taken out and put into apartments within eight or nine months. Everybody thought it was much too soon. What happened was, that that group of people, eleven families, struggled for four or five months and then suddenly they were on their own and they had their own apartments, and their own independent lives. Those who remained behind are still there [in the absorption center] five or six years later.

In part, at least, the Ethiopians' choices of housing were based on considerations they shared with most groups in the population: the availability of work, the suitability of the climate, and the centrality of the location. Thus, despite their age-old dream of living in "Jerusalem," most Ethiopians rejected the climate as too cold. Their aversion to living on the West Bank was based not on political considerations but on its relative isolation.

Their demand to live as close as possible to family members (often on the same block or in the same building) had, in contrast, more complicated roots. While based to a considerable degree on the "natural" desire to be near kin, this should not be viewed as simply the carryover of a traditional pattern. Villages in Ethiopia were widely scattered and communication and transportation were often rudimentary. A married woman residing in her husband's village might see her parents only a few times a year, her sisters even less often. Yet, despite the vast improvement in transportation and telephone communication, many Ethiopian immigrants sought to live far closer to relatives in Israel than they had in Ethiopia. This pattern may well reflect an instinctive turning to family for support in the face of the uncertainty and disruption of migration and resettlement. Many Ethiopians, it must be remembered, had lost family members or been separated from them for long periods. Significantly, perhaps, well-integrated young people were about the only Ethiopians who expressed some interest in living at a distance from family members.

As the Ethiopians became increasingly aware of their ability to stay indefinitely in temporary housing, some became reticent to leave the security of the absorption centers for permanent housing that did not meet all their needs. Further extended by interministerial squabbling, the Ethiopians' temporary sojourn in absorption centers stretched for years. At the end of 1987, almost 40 percent of those who had arrived in Operation Moses had still not been resettled. In some cases, absorption officials, rather than moving the Ethiopians into permanent housing, left the immigrants in place and simply changed the status of the absorption center by removing the services they had provided. Overnight, temporary housing designed to accommodate people on a short-term basis was decreed to be permanent housing, whose residents had to pay rent, utilities, taxes, etc. Even at the time of Operation Solomon, almost seven years after their arrival, over a thousand Ethiopians were still in absorption centers, living in temporary houses that would never be homes.

Whatever the drawbacks of the absorption centers, these pale in significance when compared to the situation of those Ethiopians placed in hotels. Squeezed into small rooms, deprived of virtually all privacy, these immigrants faced the hardest adjustment by far. While those in absorption centers had few unmediated contacts with outsiders and arranged most of their business with Israeli authorities through absorption staffers, those in hotels were deprived of almost all semblance of personal autonomy. Those in absorption centers, for example, quickly began to prepare Ethiopian food in their own kitchens to be eaten at their convenience, but hotel residents ate strange food, in a public dining hall, on a prearranged schedule. In many cases, already-vulnerable families totally ceased to function, as children learned to rely on outsiders for even such basic needs as food. At the time of Operation Moses, only a small portion of the new immigrants was housed in hotels. In response to the obvious difficulties they experienced, these families were, moreover, among the first to be resettled into permanent homes. Despite this experience, Operation Solomon, which brought an even greater number of immigrants and came in the midst of a massive *aliyah* from the Soviet Union, produced an even greater dependence on hotels. Initially over twelve thousand Ethiopian immigrants were housed in this manner, and the depressing images of passivity, dependence, and family disintegration resurfaced.

16.2.6. Three youths in their room in the Ariel hotel, Netanya, 1984. (Doron Bachar, Beth Hatefutsoth.)

In many cases immigrants were unable even to prepare a cup of coffee in their rooms.

Although it was promised that all Ethiopian immigrants would be settled in permanent housing within a year of Operation Solomon, half a year later barely 20 percent of those in hotels had been moved elsewhere. In all, over twenty thousand Ethiopian *olim* had yet to be permanently resettled. By early 1992, it had been conceded that most of these immigrants would not be given permanent housing in the foreseeable future, but would be moved instead to mobile home camps, an updated version of the *ma'abarot* of the 1950s. Here, in isolated artificial settlements whose population sometimes approached that of small towns, they await yet another move at an unspecified date.

A Struggle for Dependence?

For many Ethiopians their sojourn in Israeli absorption centers and hotels continued a pattern of dependence that had begun in either the Sudan or Addis Ababa. For months or even years, they had lived as refugees and relied on the generosity of others for their survival. Although attempts were made during the period prior to Operation Solomon to find meaningful work for as many Ethiopians as possible in Addis Ababa, their numbers and the conditions they endured made this extremely difficult. In any event, such efforts came to an end as soon as they arrived in Israel and became involved in an absorption process designed to familiarize them as quickly as possible with the language, customs, and norms of their new homeland.

Initially, virtually every move made by the new immigrants was controlled by and mediated through Jewish Agency workers. For a number of reasons the Ethiopians were all too ready to accept the cocoonlike protection they were offered. In part, at least, their responses may have been modeled on behavior found in Ethiopia, where the poor often fared better from charity than from striking out on their own.

Like refugees elsewhere in the world, moreover, Ethiopian immigrants arrived in Israel with a strong belief that, having found sanctuary, they would now be compensated for their suffering. As refugee expert Barry N. Stein has noted, refugees have a "strong belief that they are owed something by someone. Since their persecutors are unavailable, the refugees shift their demands to the government and helping agencies." Moreover, as *olim* welcomed by and cared for by the Jewish state, they carried high expectations that all their needs would be met.

At first, this was indeed the case. Not only did the various absorption agencies provide the immigrants with housing, clothing, and food, but hundreds of Israelis came forward with gifts of clothing, toys, blankets, and anything else they could think of. Following Operation Solomon, the Jewish community of France donated over 150 tons of supplies, including milk and diapers. Hadassah members brought underwear, pens, and dolls. In cases when they lived together, Soviet immigrants looked on with amazement and envy as visitors walked by them to shower gifts upon the Ethiopians. At times, the Israeli willingness to help their needy fellow Jews seemed to know no bounds. A program about Ethiopian orphans broadcast shortly after Operation Moses produced hundreds of inquiries from Israelis wishing to explore adoption.

This tremendous beneficence was, however, not without its darker side. In some instances dramatic gestures of giving seemed designed more to satisfy the donor than to assist the recipient. Thus, not once, but twice, black "cabbage patch" dolls were brought to Ethiopian children, many of whom quickly consigned them to the garbage heap. On a more serious level, while giving presents such as school supplies and toys directly to smiling Ethiopian children was immensely gratifying to both sides and provided excellent photo opportunities, it also reinforced the fact that in their new homes outsiders, not parents, were the source for both satisfying needs and obtaining luxuries.

More generally, the longer the Ethiopians were helped because they were helpless, the more habituated they became to displaying their need for charity. Some grew quite accustomed to their role as indigent wards and came to view it as natural. Thus, they felt deeply wronged when immigrant benefits such as free housing or medical care that

17.2.7. A young Ethiopian girl in Israel, Independence Day 1985.
(Doron Bachar, Beth Hatefutsoth.)

they had come to view as their right were terminated after the end of the mandated period. In the words of one Beersheva immigrant, "If we pay . . . they will also make other demands, and we are immigrants and should not have to make such payments." Even programs that called for only a symbolic financial contribution from the *olim* were often resisted. They had been loyal and obedient, so why were their benefactors "punishing" them?

Others seemed to view individual initiative as something to be hidden. The same Beersheva resident felt that "we must present ourselves not as we are, sometimes even as destitute, to get something out of them." Students often attempted to conceal the fact that they had paying jobs because they believed that scholarships were only given to the truly needy and they might be penalized for their enterprise.

Thus, while many Ethiopians in Israel struggle for independence, eking out a living in any way possible, others have learned to struggle for dependence, devoting their energies to winning the favors of the absorption agencies and charitable bodies. For those in the latter group, success is measured not by the extent of their achievements but by how much they can get from outsiders. In many cases, they are extremely successful.

As we shall see in the next few chapters, the culture of dependence that has developed among some Ethiopians has important implications for the development of their family life. This Ethiopian reliance on outsiders undermines their family's role as both a producer and a source of support. Not only do family members, particularly children, learn to look to outsiders for basic needs and luxuries, but they also come to expect immigration officials to care for relatives newly arrived in Israel. As one social worker complained, "They leave their immigrant relatives to the Sochnut or to Social Welfare. Okay they visit them, talk with them, but they don't do anything practical to help them, to get things done."

Nor were newcomers the only ones to depend on outsiders to cushion the effects of the collapse of the "safety net" usually provided by the extended family. Consider, for example, the case of Akiva Mengistu, who arrived during Operation Moses. Seven years later, while serving in the Israeli army, Akiva suddenly appeared on the front page of the Hebrew daily *Yediot Aharonot* as a "homeless" soldier who had nowhere to go on the Sabbath and holidays. Although his family had arrived in Operation Solomon, their cramped temporary quarters were too small to include yet another person. Within two days, over a thousand requests from Israelis eager to "adopt" him had arrived at the newspaper offices and had been passed on to the army's project that hosts soldiers without families. The question that remained unanswered, even unasked, was how, with forty thousand Ethiopians in the country, including two well-funded immigrant organizations and numerous members of Akiva's extended family, a young soldier from a people known for their hospitality and mutual support could end up sleeping in bus stations and abandoned houses?

Preserving Culture or Inventing Tradition?

Although we have not explicitly covered the subject of Beta Israel culture in the first three sections of this chapter, it has never been far from our discussions. Indeed, each of the topics considered above hints at one of the greatest dilemmas Ethiopians in Israel face today: How much of their distinctive culture must they surrender in order to enter into Israeli society? Whether the demands placed on the Ethiopians are precisely defined by a single authority, as in the case of the Rabbinate, or are the result of more general social forces, the challenge remains essentially the same.

In traditional Ethiopia, the Beta Israel adopted many elements from the dominant Christian culture, but retained a separate social and religious identity. In this manner they survived for hundreds of years. The challenge that confronts Ethiopian Jews in Israel is virtually a mirror image of that which they encountered in the past. Overwhelmingly, they seek to become part of the social and religious mainstream. The crucial question is, can they do this without having to abandon their own culture for that of their neighbors?

In reality, of course, the predicament they face is far more complex than a simple either/or situation. As we saw in the previous chapter, already in Ethiopia many Beta Israel had undergone changes that hinted at what awaited them in Israel. Religious practices changed, children grew more independent, the authority of elders declined, young women did not automatically marry at puberty. The clock cannot be turned back. And it is both inaccurate and hopelessly romantic to talk, as many do, of "preserving Ethiopian culture." Cultures, like fossils, are best preserved in museums. For them to live, they must be exposed to the light of day and the touch of human beings. To paraphrase the anthropologist Mary Douglas, "And if a culture is not developing, is it really a culture at all?"

The recognition that cultures always change should not, however, be read as a carte blanche to recreate the Ethiopians in the Israelis' own image. Because Israel is a country dedicated to the integration of immigrants, there is a frightening tendency to "help" newcomers fit in by explaining "how we do it here." While based largely on good intentions, one mustn't forget where those lead. The line between explaining a new culture and destroying an old one is often very thin.

Today, many Israelis are painfully aware of the fact that, in the 1950s, Jewish immigrants mainly from North Africa were pressured to abandon much of their traditional culture. All agree that immigrants should be treated with greater sensitivity, and many programs have been developed that focus on the crafts, music, and "folklore" of different ethnic groups. In the case of the Ethiopians, however, their lack of familiarity with modern technology has often led to their being labeled "primitive." At times they have been treated as empty vessels waiting to be filled. Even the most personal and idiosyncratic aspects of "civilization" are not exempt. Thus, at the time of Operation Moses, one social worker explained to a reporter, "We have to teach them everything! Why, they don't even sleep in pajamas, so I had to explain that here we sleep in pajamas." One can only wonder how large a sample she made before coming to the conclusion that most Israelis sleep in pajamas!

Israeli concern with the cultural integration of the Ethiopians has, it must be stressed, an important positive side. In comparison to most Westerners and especially Americans, Israelis are not very concerned

18.2.8. A wedding in Qiryat Arba, August 1985. Although this is a rabbinic wedding, the groom wears a traditional Ethiopian headband of red and white, symbolizing virginity and purity. (Doron Bachar, Beth Hatefutsoth.)

with the issue of skin color. The crucial categories for Israelis are Arab/Jew—Jew/non-Jew, Religious/Secular, and European/Middle Eastern. Black/white has never been an important distinction. For most Israelis, therefore, the primary strangeness of the Ethiopians is not their color but their culture: their language, their foods, their clothes, and their manners.

In the course of time, some Israelis have grown to appreciate certain aspects of Ethiopian culture. Their deep, abiding respect for older people, which we shall consider in some detail below, has impressed many outsiders. Their soft-spokenness and impeccable manners are also often contrasted favorably with Israeli curtness. In Ethiopia, to speak in a low voice is considered a sign of good family background and training. Indeed, it is often referred to as a "whispering culture". Initially at least, the Ethiopians brought such behavior with them to their new homes. The Ethiopians' protest against the Rabbinate was, for example, particularly moving because it was carried out in almost complete silence. As former American ambassador to Israel Samuel Lewis once commented, "The Israelis all seem impressed by the Ethiopians' quietness and manners. Perhaps they'll start copying it."

Both as individuals and as a group the Ethiopians must make hundreds of decisions regarding which elements of their tradition to retain, which to transform, and which to abandon. Not all aspects of their culture will be treated in the same fashion. Nor will all Ethiopians make the same decisions. Already significant differences can be seen in matters of religious observance, dress, food, and family organization.

Two aspects of the Ethiopians' attempt to define their new cultural identity will be our primary concern in the rest of this book: First, many of the cultural issues being debated, including norms of parent-child relations, gender roles, and sexual behavior, are directly related to the function and transformation of the family. Second, when family members disagree on the cultural norms they accept, the clash between cultures becomes a clash between spouses, parents and children, and the sexes. It is to these two themes that we now turn our attention.

CHAPTER THREE

Between Parent and Child:
A Generation of the Wilderness?

Having broadly considered the range of dilemmas that face both Ethiopian Jews and those working with them, we now turn our attention to the specifics of family life in their new home. As noted in the introduction to this book, the changes that have taken place in the Ethiopian Jewish family in Israel can be broadly divided into two types. On the one hand the internal structure of the family has been reorganized as age, gender, and parental authority all acquire new meanings and contexts. On the other, the family's external borders have been redrawn as many of its functions have been taken over by other institutions.

Thus, as we saw in the last chapter, marriage, which in Ethiopia was a family and communal concern, became subject to the dictates of an outside body, the Chief Rabbinate. Housing, which was intimately connected with family ties and patterns of residence, was transformed in Israel to a tug-of-war between traditional loyalties and ministerial policies. Finally, the financial independence of the family decreased in the face of an externally determined series of benefits, allowances, and market forces.

Perhaps most significantly, Ethiopian Jews in Israel encountered a series of institutions embedded in a culture whose basic definition of a "family" was radically different from their own. While extended families are, for many Israelis, more important than for most Americans, contacts beyond one or two generations (grandparents, siblings, first cousins) are often sporadic and limited to family celebrations such as weddings, funerals, etc. On a daily basis a nuclear family consisting of a father, mother, and children is the most fundamental social unit and is treated as such by outside bodies such as schools, health clinics, banks, etc.

For the Beta Israel, in contrast, social life was organized around the flexible and often-overlapping concepts of the extended family (zamad) and household (beta sa'ab). Zamad is a term whose precise meaning varies according to the circumstances and, in particular, according to what it is being contrasted. Thus, zamad is most frequently used to refer to an entire extended family (as opposed to strangers), but it was also used to distinguish blood relations (yesaga zamad) from in-laws (amachenat). When searching for a spouse for a son or daughter, parents would automatically exclude anyone in their zamad counting back seven generations. Thus to marry even a third cousin would be considered a form of incest! Since sons traditionally settled in the same village as their parents when they married, many local communities consisted of one or several extended families. Membership in a large and powerful zamad provided both practical benefits and social standing. Members of a zamad were expected to support each other in time of need. Within the borders of the zamad little attention was paid to the "real" relationship between members. Thus, according to the circumstances, grandparents, uncles, or older siblings might be a child's "parents." A person's "children" might easily include nieces, nephews, stepchildren, and younger siblings. His or her biological sons and daughters might be teens before they realized that some of their "brothers and sisters" were in fact cousins!

In contrast to the geographically dispersed zamad, which was reckoned over seven generations, the beta sa'ab (household) was a residential unit whose membership changed over time. Although often composed around a core nuclear family, widowed parents, divorced siblings, elderly relatives, various children, and even servants were

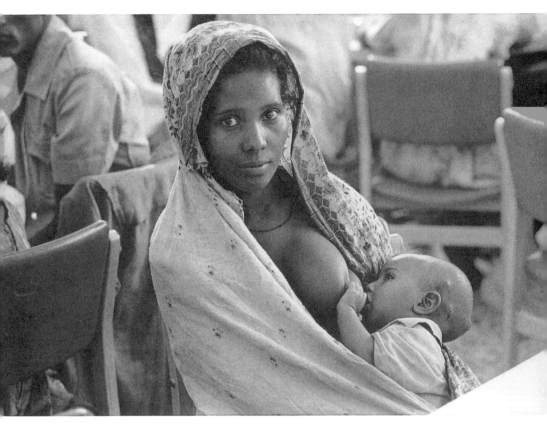

19.3.1. Mother and child, Ashqelon, 1984. (Doron Bachar, Beth Hatefutsoth.)

often vital parts of a single *beta sa'ab*. At any given moment, the precise configuration of the *beta sa'ab* was determined by an assortment of personal preferences and needs and would change as these changed.

The relationship between the *zamad* and *beta sa'ab* is well illustrated by the case of S'doto, today a student at Hebrew University in Jerusalem.

> Before she married my father, my mother had a different husband. She had a daughter and I went to live with her [at age nine] in Wollo. She [the half-sister] had daughters, but no sons, so she wanted someone to come and be their brother, like a brother. I am their cousin [sic!]. Also I was their age, so I was like their brother. . . . So I went and I grew up in Wollo and studied until twelfth grade.

S'doto's half-sister and her daughters are all part of his *zamad*. At age nine, he left his nuclear family to join his half-sister's *beta sa'ab* (which also included his maternal grandmother). One major consideration appears to have been the fact that she had no sons. Since he was approximately the same age as his half-nieces, he was treated as their brother.

Under the best of circumstances, situations such as S'doto's would have tested the limits of Israeli institutions geared to operate around a nuclear family. How is one, for example, to reckon the number of children in each family? Should S'doto be counted with his nuclear family, whom he left eleven years ago, or with the household in which he grew up? Should a younger child in his situation be treated as an orphan if his or her biological parents are absent, but the senior members of his or her household are present? Moreover, the additional disruptions that resulted from separation, death, divorce, and remarriage made even such "normal" families an exception among Ethiopian Jews in Israel.

From Elders to Golden-Agers

If the terms *zamad* and *beta sa'ab* reveal one manner in which Ethiopian ideas about the family differ from those of many Israelis, the concept of *shmagile* (elder) reveals yet another. In contrast to the avowedly child- and youth-centered norms of Israeli society, the Beta Israel of Ethiopia respected and honored the elderly and aged. As a man grew older, his personal status grew. The appearance of his first grey hairs was a source of pride, not of discomfort or embarrassment. If he was well thought of and behaved honorably, he would be considered a *shmagile* by the time he reached his late thirties or early forties. The word itself carried with it connotations of respect and reverence.

The *shmagile* was an arbitrator of the norms of Beta Israel society. People came to him with their problems and asked for his advice. Unhappy couples, quarreling in-laws, and feuding neighbors would all come to him for guidance. When dealing with major problems, the individual *shmagile* did not act alone, but in concert with an informal council of both *shmagilotch* (elders) and *qessotch* (priests). Together they settled disputes between villages, served as witnesses to important events, and represented their local communities to outsiders. As Joseph Halévy wrote after visiting the Beta Israel in 1868, "Justice is exercised by the elders *(chimaguelié)*. Complaints and disputes are brought before them. Their decisions are always respected by both parties."

Although the *shmagilotch* were exclusively men, older women also had an important role to play. A senior woman, particularly one who had reached menopause, was referred to as a *baaltet*. In this capacity, she was considered to be well versed in issues relating to women, including childbirth and certain illnesses. While she lacked the community-wide prestige of her male counterpart, she too might be called upon to arbitrate a dispute, particularly between younger women.

The Beta Israel's respect for age was not limited to their community's elders. Children were expected to act with reserve and quiet respect toward all adults, particularly their parents and the head of their extended family *(zamad)*. Even elder siblings were treated with deference. Thus, children were usually fed *after* the adults. When a child spoke with elders, he or she was expected to raise his or her voice no louder than a barely audible whisper and to use the polite forms of address that characterize Amharic. In contrast, older men would often address their teenage relatives as *ashkar* (servant)!

20.3.2. *Shmagile* (elder), Ethiopia, 1991. (Robert Lyons © 1991.)

As we saw in an earlier chapter, the status of parents and elders in Ethiopia had begun to decline even before the revolution of 1974. In Marxist Ethiopia, this process continued at an even faster pace. The generation gap separating the young (some of whom were strongly influenced by the new government's teachings) and the elders grew. Young leaders challenged the traditional norms of decision making and mediation, and some participated to an unprecedented degree in outside political and social organizations.

These changes notwithstanding, the elders were able to retain a modicum of authority as long as the Beta Israel remained in Ethiopia. Their experience in handling the day-to-day problems of village life remained a valuable commodity. Once they reached Israel, however, their situation deteriorated rapidly. Faced with unprecedented challenges in a strange new society, their years of accumulated wisdom suddenly seemed irrelevant. Settled haphazardly around the country, the reputation for sound judgment they had earned through years of shrewd arbitration on a local village level appeared to evaporate.

No less important in their loss of status was the essential foreignness of the concept of the *shmagile* to the (predominantly young) absorption officials. For immigration agencies, the elderly, far from being a source of wisdom and advice, are something of a problem. Frequently referred to in Israel by the Biblical term "the generation of the wilderness," mature adult and elderly immigrants are viewed as a portion of the population that can never really be successful integrated into the new society.

The impact of this bias against the elderly is best revealed by a remarkable bit of cross-cultural mistranslation that took place at the time of Operation Moses. Told that Ethiopian men in their early forties became "elders," absorption officials quickly interpreted this to mean that they retired from active involvement in economic and communal affairs. Thus the respected and honored *shmagile* was transformed into a "golden-ager" more suited for occupational therapy than useful employment. A generation of men on the threshold of elderhood suddenly found themselves thrust aside.

The peripheralization of the *shmagilotch* was significant not only for its impact on the elders themselves but also for its effect on the

21.3.3. *Qessotch* (priests) at Judaism seminar, Nir Etzion, 1984.
(Doron Bachar, Beth Hatefutsoth.)

community as a whole. Although several groups of young Ethiopians came forward in an attempt to seize the political leadership of the community, none was able to fill the social void created by the loss of the *shmagilotch*. Thus, at precisely the time when the Ethiopian community was experiencing some of its greatest difficulties, one of its most important institutions for dealing with crisis was in ruins.

Gradually and rather hesitantly, small groups of social workers and other absorption workers began to consult and mobilize *shmagilotch* in their dealings with community members. In some cases directors of absorption centers even organized councils of elders with whom they held regular consultations. In the most ambitious such project, Betachin (in Amharic: Our House), a family counseling and mediation center operated by the Joint Distribution Committee, employs a number of Ethiopian staffers, including laymen and *qessotch*, to help resolve family problems. Less formally, but probably in far greater numbers, Ethiopians have continued to turn to their elders for advice in times of distress.

Between Parent and Child

Nowhere are the internal and external transformations undergone by Ethiopian families in Israel more obvious than in parent-child relations. Much of what we have described above concerning the decline of the *shmagile* on the communal level also applies to the status of parents. Thus changes already "in the air" in prerevolutionary Ethiopia were dramatically accelerated by both events in Ethiopia and the *aliyah* process.

For many young Beta Israel their childhood ended when they left their villages for the Sudan or Addis Ababa. Thousands of those who emigrated during the early 1980s left behind one or even both parents. In many cases, seven years passed before they met again. Many others were deprived of even this delayed reunion. Avraham, a veteran immigrant whose father died when he was a child, lost his mother after he made *aliyah*. "She died in Ethiopia . . . my mother died when they started *aliyah* through Sudan. . . . I heard about her when people from our village started to come . . . and they told me about her. . . . When I heard about my mother's death, the whole world fell to pieces."

For those who survived, challenges of a different kind lay ahead. As we saw above, the sojourn in Addis Ababa put great strain on the Ethiopian family. Although Operation Solomon changed this, the move to Israeli hotels offered challenges of a new kind. Similarly, while it ended years of separation for many family members, their physical reunification was often the occasion for graphic demonstrations of the tremendous differences that had developed between the newcomers and their "Israeli" relatives. Nowhere was this clearer than in the case of parents preceded by their children. Social worker Danny Budowski, who works counseling Ethiopian families at Betachin, describes a typical scenario:

> If you have a boy who has been here for eight years and his father has come, the father would expect him to behave in an Ethiopian manner, blessing him, giving him honor, and acting to him like he would in Ethiopia. But here sometimes the kid would shake his hand with one hand and not with two hands, would not bend [as a sign of respect] in a proper manner, would be hasty in speech, would not have the patience he used to have. He would go up and ask the father questions instead of waiting for the father to ask him . . . these kind of things could raise quite a few tensions.

Nor were such difficulties limited to those families that had experienced separation. Among Ethiopians in Israel, as among most immigrant groups, children tend to adapt more quickly and completely than their parents. Accordingly, while young Ethiopians have generally learned Hebrew with alacrity and have quickly grasped the workings of Israeli society, their elders have often gained only the most minimal skills in the new language and remain mystified by the world around them. In some cases, traditional roles are almost completely reversed as children assume the primary responsibility for representing the family to the outside world. Then, as Ethiopian-born educator Rahamim Yitzhak, who runs programs for Ethiopian parents, notes, "The child starts to think about his father . . . 'he doesn't understand. And without me, he can't do anything. I'm the translator for his family doctor, for his social security, and without me [he can't do anything]. In Ethiopia I respected him . . . here I know everything. . . . ' Then the friction starts within the family."

No less significantly, the youngsters' acceptance of Israeli norms has usually been more rapid than that of their parents. Frequently, this places them in a terrible bind: the more successfully they pursue their natural desire to integrate and become like their non-Ethiopian friends and classmates, the greater the distance between them and their parents. While some strive and manage to achieve a precarious balance, acting Israeli in the street and Ethiopian at home, others find themselves torn between two sets of seemingly irreconcilable cultural norms.

Between Parent and Student

The challenges facing Ethiopian parents in Israel are most starkly revealed in their contacts with their children's schools. In contrast to the usual pattern in Israel, whereby many of their traditional functions and responsibilities are handed over to outside agencies, here they are (at least in theory) being asked to assume a new role as "parents-of-students."

It is difficult to overestimate the challenge this new role poses for most Ethiopian parents. Despite the claims of recent Ethiopian governments that the country's educational system has been greatly improved and expanded, most of the adults who arrived in Israel had no formal schooling before they attended Ulpan (Hebrew language) classes. While their period in the Ulpan served to familiarize them with many of the basics of the classroom situation—books, notebooks, pencils, blackboards, etc.—it only gave them a limited sense of the intricacies of the school system as a whole. (In fact, even after a year many adults, in contrast to their children, had failed to achieve even a basic working command of Hebrew.) Not only were the demands of the Ulpan far more limited than that of regular studies, but also, as with most aspects of absorption-center life, virtually all of the technical arrangements were handled by staff members. Few Ethiopian parents, for example, can be said to have gained an understanding of such matters as grading systems or homework assignments during their period in Ulpan.

The entry of the Ethiopian students into the Israeli school system in the wake of Operation Moses was difficult for all involved. Although given time to prepare, the Israel Ministry of Education had made few plans for this influx. As the Israel state comptroller noted, "[It] began to gear itself—with regard to preparing cadres of teachers, curricula, and syllabi, and drawing up an overall policy—very late, after the [Ethiopian] children were already attending school. Even then, the pace was very slow." One direct consequence of this lapse was that most Ethiopian parents sent their children off to school with little sense of the norms or expectations under which they operated. For their part, the teachers and school staff had little sense of what needed to be explained. Tardiness, inadequate dress, unkempt appearance, a lack of supplies (pencils, notebooks), and insufficient lunches were only a few of the problems which developed at the outset. Nor were Ethiopian parents, particularly those living in absorption centers, likely to venture out to the strange world of the school to investigate their children's progress.

At first glance, such behavior could easily be interpreted as a sign that Ethiopians do not value education or, at least, that they had failed to recognize its importance. Nothing could be further from the truth. In fact, once in the classroom Ethiopian students tended to be not only well behaved and quiet but also highly motivated and disciplined. Parents and students alike questioned the need for breaks and outside activities such as *tiyulim* (hikes), when there was so much serious learning to do.

In many cases, difficulties appeared to result from the fact that Ethiopian parents had never had the schools' expectations explained to them. In others instances, these expectations seemed either bizarre or unfair, or both. What, for example, was one to make of a system that first required you to send your child to school and then expected you to both purchase supplies and pay for certain programs? Even had their resources not been limited, and had they not become accus-

22.3.4. Mother nursing child during Ulpan class, King Saul Hotel, Ashqelon, 1985. (Doron Bachar, Beth Hatefutsoth.)

tomed to receiving so much for free, such demands would have been difficult to accept.

Ultimately, however, the "mechanical" aspects of school attendance, such as punctuality, neatness, the purchase of supplies, and the packing of a lunch, are no harder to learn than the mechanical use of unfamiliar appliances like refrigerators and toasters. Such problems rarely persisted for very long. Other difficulties were far harder to resolve. Even when Ethiopian parents understand the purpose and importance of homework, for example, few are capable of assisting with it. The most common solution to this problem is to provide tutors, either individually or, more commonly, for groups of Ethiopian children at community centers. Such programs are a vital supplement to the regular studies of many young Ethiopians. Indeed, one testimony to their success is the fact that by the time of Operation Solomon, the tutors were themselves often Ethiopian "graduates" of such programs. By taking the "home" out of homework, however, such programs inevitably exclude parents from yet another aspect of the student's life.

Indeed, from the Ethiopian parents' perspective, formal education is noteworthy first and foremost for the manner in which it reduces the child's link to his or her family. For the first time in living experience, children's daily lives no longer revolve around their household and kin. Most of their time is spent outside the home in a world both physically and *culturally* distant from that of their parents. Moreover, while most Ethiopian students usually spend their first year with other Ethiopians in special *kitot kelet* (absorption classes), thereafter they are expected to study in regular classes with other Israelis. By their second year, therefore, they are increasingly taking their behavior cues from their classmates and peers.

In and of itself, this situation is normal and even desirable. The ability to get along with those outside one's immediate family is one of the most important lessons that schools have to teach. In the case of Ethiopian immigrants, however, several important points should be kept in mind. First, the norms that Ethiopian children are exposed to in school, including the infinite little details that make up daily behavior—how one greets friends, answers a teacher, requests assis-

23.3.5. Ethiopian child in school, Atlit, 1984. (Doron Bachar, Beth Hatefutsoth.)

tance, etc.—are often greatly at odds with those of Ethiopia and their parents. Relations between teachers and students in Israel are, for example, quite informal. Teachers are addressed by their first names and often attempt to cultivate a friendly and relaxed relationship with their students. When Ethiopian children attempt such behavior with their elders at home, it appears rude and disrespectful.

Second, even when parents and adults are themselves open to such new cultural norms, their exposure to them is relatively limited in comparison with that of their children. Few frameworks available to Ethiopian adults revolve as completely around contact with Israelis and Israeli culture as do their children's schools. Thus, even when parents and children are moving in the same direction, when the latters' "natural" ability to adjust more quickly is combined with the unique intensity of the school experience, a gap in their rate of adjustment usually develops.

In the case of the Ethiopians, moreover, the elements absorbed at school involve not only informal rules of daily behavior but also central elements of normative religious practice. Under a policy established when the first groups of Ethiopians began to arrive in Israel, all Ethiopian children are sent to religious schools. The official justification for this policy is that, having come from traditional religious backgrounds, Ethiopians will suffer less "culture shock" in religious schools. As we have already seen, such labels as "traditional" and "religious" often mask a far more complex reality. Despite the changes that began in Ethiopia, a wide gap often separates Beta Israel religious life from that which they encounter in Israel. Moreover, and this is of direct concern, immersion in the religious school system often means that children are exposed to, understand, and adopt elements of "normative" Judaism much more quickly than their parents. Religious knowledge, one of the foundation stones of traditional communal life, becomes yet another element no longer under the definitive control of *qessotch*, elders, and parents.

Youth Aliyah

All of the processes described above appear in an even more exaggerated form when Ethiopian teenagers are placed in boarding schools run by Youth Aliyah (Aliyat Hanoar). Youth Aliyah was founded in 1932 by Henrietta Szold. In 1933 it accepted its first group of parentless children from Germany. Many others were to follow in their wake. During the period of the massive *aliyah* from the Middle East and North Africa, most of the immigrant children placed in Youth Aliyah institutions had parents in the country, but were removed from their homes to speed their acculturation. When large-scale *aliyah* ceased, Youth Aliyah then turned its attention to Israeli children from broken homes and deprived backgrounds. At the time of Operation Moses, most of those in Youth Aliyah institutions were children from such families.

By the 1980s considerable misgivings existed concerning attempts in the 1950s to speed the absorption of immigrant youths by separating them from their families. It was accordingly decided to consider each case of the Ethiopians on an individual basis. In the end, over 96 percent of Ethiopian children who arrived in the 1980s were placed in youth villages!

One cannot exaggerate the benefits this offered them or the energy invested in them. At the time of Operation Moses, faced with an influx of over a thousand Ethiopians whose parents were not in the country, Youth Aliyah workers scoured the country in an attempt to locate other family members. From the outset, every effort was made to create an environment in which Ethiopian youths would feel safe, secure, and encouraged to be proud of their heritage. Moreover, some of the most innovative programs for Ethiopians in such areas as psychological counseling and health education were developed under Youth Aliyah auspices.

Small wonder, therefore, that even when Operation Solomon had reunified most families and largely eliminated the most widely accepted justification for sending children to boarding schools, Ethiopian teens continued to be targeted to Youth Aliyah. The explana-

24.3.6. Ethiopian boys in computer course at Mikve Israel, Youth Aliyah boarding school, 1986. (Doron Bachar, Beth Hatefutsoth.)

tions varied, and often came from veteran Ethiopians themselves. Some noted, for example, that, already in Ethiopia, the small percentage of children who went to high school usually left their homes and villages, so boarding schools were in a sense "traditional." Others argued, on a more practical level, that the combination of large families and small apartments meant that Ethiopian teens rarely had a quiet place to study at home. What better solution than to accept a place in a boarding school? After all, some even claimed, harking back to the "generation of the wilderness" concept, living with their parents would only slow down the children's acculturation.

Whatever their reasons, many Ethiopians show what seems to outsiders an almost unseemly willingness to send their older children to Youth Aliyah schools, or to attend them themselves. In one case in late 1991, a mother was reunited with her teenage son, whom she had left behind in Ethiopia seven years earlier. In front of numerous reporters and photographers at Ben Gurion Airport, they held an emotional and tearful reunion. Motivated by either her concern for his education or a lack of space in her apartment, she waited less than a week to contact Youth Aliyah and ask that they find a place for him as soon as possible!

More commonly, young adults eager to enter boarding schools attempted to get around the age limits set by the educational bureaucracy by claiming to be in their teens. In some cases, young couples without children even separated to meet the entrance requirement that students be unmarried.

Despite their obvious success and popularity, Youth Aliyah's schools remain the subject of much controversy. While few doubted the short-term benefits to children, some questioned the long-term effects on the family of the boarding school option. In the light of experiences with previous *olim*, wouldn't so widespread a use of boarding schools once again leave immigrant teens with few links to the local population and no family roots? Rahamim Yitzhak describes, for example, the potential impact of the child's rapid acculturation on a family:

> He feels more Israeli if he goes to the boarding school. He likes to live like an Israeli. He likes to behave like an Israeli. He likes to talk like an Israeli. But culturally in the home, it's sometimes not accepted. . . .

Education can be divided into two types: formal and informal. And if you disconnect the child from the informal [family] education, what have you done? The control of the father will be less. And the result will be very bad. . . . When he lives with me [at home], I teach him as a father, and my wife teaches him as a mother. I'm afraid we've been missing that part.

Hidden behind this cautious criticism, are deeper and more troubling questions: Where are the Ethiopian immigrant children of today going to find models for establishing their own families? How can such young adults who have spent their teens in Youth Aliyah boarding schools and the next three years in the armed forces be expected to strike roots in local communities and create stable homes for the next generation? By educating them in a setting far removed from their parents and families, doesn't Youth Aliyah take the double risk of creating both a senior "generation of the wilderness" and a rootless younger generation in which, to paraphrase the Bible, "every man does that which is right in his own eyes" (Judges 21:25)?

Ethiopian Jews in Israel have entered a society whose basic definitions of family are strikingly different from those they left behind. Institutional policies focus on nuclear families rather than the *zamad* (extended family) or *beta sa'ab* (household). Youth is valued rather than age, so *shmagilotch* (elders) who acted as respected mediators and advisors in Ethiopia become neglected pensioners. Priorities tend to be determined by child-centered criteria rather than those focusing on the needs of grownups. Thus, many adults are dismissed as a "generation of the wilderness," who will never really be at home in the Promised Land. While their children attend school and become immersed in the language, values, and customs of their new homes, parents generally lag behind and struggle with a variety of challenges, including their new role as parents of students. Almost all those in their teens live and study in Youth Aliyah boarding schools, further isolating them from parental influence and models.

CHAPTER FOUR

Changing Gender Roles

Honorary Males

In our discussion of parent-child relations in the last chapter, we intentionally ignored some of the special tensions that arise for those rearing daughters in Israel. In these cases, the gap separating Ethiopian and Israeli norms concerning age and youth grows even wider because of differing views of the roles appropriate to males and females. As with parenting and childhood, the differences that divide the two cultures over gender concern both roles within the family and the border dividing the family from the outside world.

In Israel, Ethiopian women (like their children) are encouraged to take a greater role in the running of the family and to have more responsibility and autonomy in their dealings with the society around them. In Ethiopia, women traditionally deferred to men, who held all positions of authority and power. Typically, this hierarchy was expressed in the most basic elements of daily behavior. Thus, if an Ethiopian man entered a room, Ethiopian etiquette required that everyone, men *and women,* rise and remain standing until he accepted a seat or left. The social nicety of "ladies first" is not a part of the Ethiopian cultural pattern. Men are "first," "more important," and, in general, more respected by both sexes. Within the family, a woman's responsibilities were generally limited to the domestic realm.

25.4.1. Ethiopian woman, Gondar region, 1991. (Robert Lyons ©
1991.)

The Ethiopian male's encounter with a new set of gender roles begins in the first minute of the absorption process. The workers at the center—*ulpan* teachers, social workers, house mothers, etc.—are predominantly women. Ethiopian etiquette dictates that he show respect to such authority figures; it also dictates that they, as women, defer to him. The solution to this seemingly irreconcilable conflict is to deny the female absorption worker's gender. To quote Israeli psychologist Gadi Ben Ezer, "A female authority figure, from his viewpoint, is not a woman. He ceases to react to her as a woman, and for him she is solely an authority figure, a representative of the government, and therefore to be honored."

Such "desexualization" of non-Ethiopian women did not originate in Israel. It had precedents in Ethiopia. Kay Kaufman Shelemay, author of *Music, Ritual, and Falasha History*, reports her experience as a "marginal male" while doing fieldwork among the Beta Israel just prior to the Ethiopian revolution of 1974:

> I encountered few problems related to my sex. Foreign women tend to be freer of many constraints imposed on Ethiopian women in traditional society; in addition, the seemingly sophisticated recording equipment I carried elevated my status. . . . Except for brief conversations with the wife of one Ambober [the largest Beta Israel village in the Gondar region] priest, my time was spent among the men. I was included in such male events as special drinking parties on Sabbath afternoons and was served with the men when eating in a private home. Village women and children touched women isolated in special huts during menstruation, but I was not allowed to approach. Although I had been advised to wear a skirt, Falasha men encouraged me to wear slacks and seemed more comfortable when I did so.

While conferring the status of "honorary" male on women absorption workers may have settled the problem of conflicting rules of etiquette, it did nothing to resolve much bigger differences concerning the proper role of women. Publicity photos of female soldiers and women *chalutzot* (pioneers) notwithstanding, Israel has, in general, been far less influenced by the feminist movement than the United States or Western Europe. Traditional cultural and religious norms remain strong in many communities and deeply embedded in many of the country's laws and customs. This conservatism notwithstanding, the average Israeli's expectations of a woman's role differ vastly from the ideals of traditional Beta Israel society.

Out of the Hut/Into the Closet

No aspect of traditional Ethiopian behavior pertaining to women has evoked as much comment and controversy in Israel as the purity laws surrounding menstruation and childbirth. In the not too distant past, laws connected with ritual purity formed a major part of Beta Israel life. Ideally, for example, all contacts with non-Beta Israel were supposed to be followed by isolation and immersion. Other persons considered impure and required to submit to ritual purification were women during menstruation and after childbirth, anyone who came in contact with a corpse or dead animal, someone who performed a circumcision, and a priest who had had sexual relations.

By the middle of the twentieth century most of these practices had slipped into disuse. Those affecting women, however, continued to survive. According to these rules, a menstruating woman would leave her home and enter a small hut at the edge of the village known as a *yamargam gojo* (hut of the curse) or *yadem gojo* (hut of blood). She would remain there at least seven days. A circle of stones surrounding the hut marked the area into which only children and other women could enter. At the end of her seclusion the woman would immerse herself in a nearby stream or river and wash her clothes. Unlike comparable customs among most Jewish communities, Beta Israel laws applied not only to married women but also to unmarried girls, divorcees, and even female servants. They were, it appears, concerned with a far stricter definition of purity than one limited to the marital realm. Thus, the woman's physical seclusion was considered necessary, lest her presence pollute the entire house.

A similar but lengthier form of seclusion was also practiced at childbirth. With the onset of labor a woman would enter the menstrual hut accompanied by two senior women who would assist her during the birth. (Their contact with the infant and mother rendered them impure and they had to undergo purification before rejoining

26.4.2. Woman sitting outside menstrual hut, Ethiopia, 1984. (Doron Bachar, Beth Hatefutsoth.)

the community.) If the child was a boy, he would be circumcised on the eighth day unless this was the Sabbath. The Beta Israel did not perform circumcisions on the Sabbath, but postponed them until sunset and the end of the festival. (The circumciser, too, is considered impure and must undergo purification.) Following the circumcision the mother washes herself, the child, and their clothes before entering the *yaras bet,* the childbirth hut, where they remain for a further thirty-two days. In the case of a female infant, the mother usually remains in the menstrual hut for two weeks, and then spends a further sixty-six days in the birth hut. Only after the completion of either forty or eighty days are mother and child both immersed and the child named.

The tenacity with which the Beta Israel have held to these customs, while abandoning or changing many others, should serve as a warning against any simple interpretation of their meaning and function. Thus neither a feminist critique attacking the customs as a symbol of the "double oppression" of Beta Israel women (as both Jews and women), nor a romantic approach defending them as a vacation away from all daily cares does justice to their complex nature. Michelle Schoenberger, an anthropologist who lived among the Beta Israel in the early 1970s, strikes a nice balance when she writes concerning menstrual separation, "Although it is not seen in this manner by the members of the society, these seven days of complete rest are important to the physical well-being of the women in Falasha society."

Given the hard physical labor that was the daily lot of Beta Israel women, the days spent in the menstrual hut may well have provided a welcome respite. Moreover, since at any given moment several women were often in seclusion, their separation from their usual obligations and male society may well have offered them a particularly good opportunity to talk and form bonds. (In this context, it is also worth noting that a married woman usually lived in her husband's village, where she was, at least at first, a relative stranger without friends.)

These positive aspects notwithstanding, the custom should not be overly idealized. However welcome the sojourn in the menstrual hut may have been as a break from hard work, seven days in this flimsy structure was scarcely a vacation. The woman was, for example, far more exposed to the elements, particularly during the rainy seasons. Her location, at the edge of a settled area, may even have made intrusions of wild animals a reasonable fear.

Even more importantly, as Schoenberger points out, while this custom may have functioned to the benefit of women in some respects, this was not its primary purpose. First and foremost, the Beta Israel viewed their observance of this ritual as yet one more example of their intense devotion to the laws of the Orit (Torah). This was important in and of itself, but also because it distinguished them from their Christian neighbors. It was, in some respects, a vital marker that separated Jews from Christians in much the same way that the refusal to eat pork (forbidden to both groups in Ethiopia) symbolized the difference between Jews and Christians in many Western countries. Beta Israel in Ethiopia looked upon the Christians' refusal to remove menstruating women from their houses not as a mere curiosity, but as a clear indication of the latter's impurity and lower moral status. Finally, as with many taboos relating to purity, Beta Israel laws carried with them an almost magic element that threatened to bring down ruin on those who violated them.

Although the Beta Israel resolutely resisted most attempts to reform their rules concerning menstrual purity, some changes did take place in Ethiopia. As we noted above, the laws of seclusion applied not only to married women but to any girl who had reached puberty. So long as most girls were married, or at least were engaged by the time they matured, this distinction was of little significance. By the late 1960s and early 1970s, however, some girls, interested in pursuing their education and/or *aliyah* to Israel, had delayed their marriages for several years. While most of these were still willing to enter the *yadem gojo*—and Jewish Agency schools made allowances for this—some refused. Moreover, it was generally understood that any girl who was allowed to continue her education outside of the village in Addis Ababa or Gondar would not be observing these (or many other) rituals. Thus, while still observed by an overwhelming majority of Beta Israel women, even these laws had ceased to be universally followed.

Despite their stated commitment to cultural pluralism, the Israeli absorption authorities made it clear from the outset that the Ethiopians would not be encouraged to retain the seclusion of women. No facilities comparable to birth or menstrual huts were provided in absorption centers. A similar policy was followed in Youth Aliyah schools, as anthropologist Shalva Weil recounts:

> I followed girls who refused to go to study. They said that they were feeling ill for a week or so. . . . The teachers caught on, that it was the girl students who were away from studies for exactly a week once a month. . . . They had to find some sort of solution. The truth of the matter is that the Ethiopian women and teenagers . . . have to adapt to the norms in Israeli society, particularly in this case.

While it is easy to dismiss such decisions as ethnocentric, the reasons behind them are far more complex and relate to many of the broader changes in family life discussed above. The Ethiopian custom was, for example, rooted in a social and economic system that, as we have seen, revolved around the extended family and the household. While a woman was in seclusion, others from her family carried out her domestic duties and cared for her children. Without this kind of broad support, how was this gap to be filled for a week, let alone forty or eighty days? Were employers and educators to allow Ethiopian women to absent themselves from work or school 25 percent of the time while demanding regular attendance from others?

The discontinuation of the menstrual separation has not been easy. Many women still observe a degree of seclusion by utilizing their apartment's balcony, the hotel corridor, or even a closet! Others, while seemingly resigned to the change, express feelings of guilt for "polluting" their families and suffer from insomnia and depression. Only a small number seem to have found a solution to their problem in adopting rabbinic laws of *niddah* and using the *mikve*. This is scarcely surprising since the two sets of rules differ in several crucial respects. First, as was noted above, while modern *niddah* observances center on sexual purity among married women, Beta Israel laws are concerned with the general separation of all menstruating women. Second, while Beta Israel custom dictated purification in a body of moving water, current Jewish practice involves immersion in the *mikve*, a pool-like ritual bath. Third, according to Beta Israel tradition a woman was separated for seven days, unless her period lasted longer. In contrast, the laws of *niddah* require a women to refrain from sexual activity from the time she expects her period (which is assumed to last at least five days) until she observes no blood for seven days. Thus the minimum period of observance is twelve days.

In contrast to their generally straightforward rejection of rabbinic norms of menstrual purity, the Ethiopians' handling of childbirth customs in Israel is far more complex. While some elements of their tradition have been almost completely abandoned, others have been retained or transformed.

The customary separation of a woman for forty or eighty days after birth is, if anything, less feasible in Israel than her separation for a week when menstruating. It has, therefore, been largely abandoned. Significantly, however, many families retain the custom of holding celebrations on the appropriate days to mark what would have been the end of the mother's and child's isolation. Such festivities are often far more lavish than those held at the time of a boy's circumcision, the usual Israeli occasion for such celebration. Indeed, since many older Ethiopians avoid seeing their daughter and grandchild for a period of forty or eighty days, in keeping with tradition, such celebrations mark the reunification of the family and its first gathering with the new infant present. It also appears likely that most couples attempt to refrain from contact as much as possible during this period, including abstinence from sexual relations.

In Israel, circumcisions can only be performed by a properly registered, rabbinically approved *mohel* (ritual circumciser). The ritual is performed in public at home or in a hall rented for the purpose, and not in a separate, isolated enclosure. Italian researcher Emanuela Trevisan Semi describes her own experience at one such ceremony in 1984:

> Traditional Beta Israel food was served . . . but apart from that, everything proceeded according to the usages of rabbinic Judaism in Israel: the mother gave the baby boy to his father, who in turn gave him to the *sandek* (godfather) who was a kinsman. (In Ethiopia, of course, a woman and her newborn baby would have been in isolation for forty

days and any person coming into direct contact with her would have been contaminated.) At the end of the ceremony a glass of wine was blessed by the *mohel* and we all in turn took a sip from it, the mother last of all. She was visibly embarrassed and stood at the threshold of the room trying to distance herself as far as she could.

While it is comparatively easy to find out how Ethiopians have handled new norms governing menstruation, childbirth, and circumcision of boys, the subject of female circumcision remains something of a taboo. In the past, the Beta Israel of Ethiopia, like many of their neighbors, performed clitorectomies on infant girls. The ceremony appears to have no fixed day, and in contrast to male circumcision did not have any Biblical sanction. It was custom, not a commandment, and was usually justified as a means of restraining a girl's sexuality, so that she would remain chaste until marriage. Already in Ethiopia, the custom had significantly declined in recent years.

Ethiopian Jews in Israel are well aware that this practice is considered taboo and unacceptable and prefer not to talk about it. Does it continue in Israel? Perhaps in isolated cases, but certainly not as a rule.

Woman at Work

While the decline of traditional purity laws is certainly the most exotic transition undergone by Ethiopian women in Israel, their entry into the work force is probably the challenge with the greatest long-term consequences. Here, too, the tensions between Ethiopian norms and those of Israel have implications not only for the women themselves but also for their relationships with their spouses and children.

In Ethiopia, a rigid gender-based division of labor existed. Women's activities included cleaning, cooking, embroidery, caring for young children, bringing water, washing clothes, making clay vessels for eating and cooking, and weaving straw baskets for storage. Men were responsible for building the family home, farming, smithing, weaving cloth, and any endeavor associated with the outside world. The two realms neatly complemented each other. Men would plough the field,

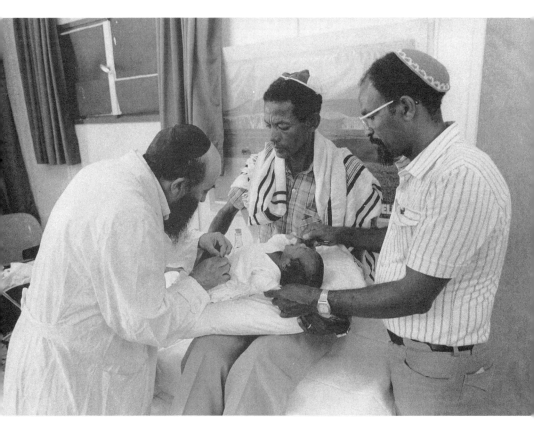

27.4.3. Circumcision ceremony at an absorption center, 1984. (Doron Bachar, Beth Hatefutsoth.)

28.4.4. Woman making *injera* (Ethiopian bread), 1991. (Robert Lyons © 1991.)

sow the seeds, protect the crops, gather and winnow the harvest, but only women would prepare the food. Men would weave cloth, but women would sew and embroider clothes. The division was usually strictly observed and it would be unthinkable for a women to perform most male tasks or for a man to perform "woman's work." Thus a single or divorced man would inevitably find a woman—a relative, a servant, or other available woman—to cook and clean for him.

Prior to the introduction of formal education, there was not a major age-based division of labor. The activities of boys and girls, once they passed the age of infancy, were largely similar to those of their parents. Boys would accompany the men to the fields and assist them in their work. Girls remained at home with their mothers and grandmothers and learned the basic skills expected of them as women and wives.

Although the distinctions drawn by the Beta Israel were essentially the same as those observed by their neighbors, Ethiopia's ethnic division of labor introduced some slight but significant differences. In contrast to their Christian counterparts, Beta Israel women were known for making clay pots. This form of work, although symbolically associated with the domestic realm and the home, was not restricted to personal use and supplemented the family income.

Initially, Ethiopian women brought to Israel were relieved of some of their domestic responsibilities. Hotels, in particular, assumed most of the work associated with the preparation of food. Even when they had moved to permanent housing many of their former daily chores, including preparing dishes and pots, fetching water, and weaving baskets, were rendered obsolete. Nevertheless, the basic ethos remained the same: Whatever was done in the house was considered the responsibility of the woman.

While the domestic realm remained restricted to women, women were no longer restricted to the domestic realm. Indeed, both ideological and practical pressures were brought to bear on Ethiopian women to explore the options for work outside the house.

As is often the case, different Israeli institutions appear to be working at cross-purposes, or at least to be looking at the subject from radi-

29.4.5. Woman shopping in supermarket, Safed, 1985. (Doron Bachar, Beth Hatefutsoth.)

cally different perspectives. Representatives of the Employment Service and other offices concerned with finding jobs for Ethiopian immigrants point to the relatively high rate of unemployment among Ethiopian women. Quite naturally, given their responsibilities, they relate to these *olot* (female immigrants) as part of the work force and see joblessness as a major problem. Their chief concern appears to be with strategies by which it may be overcome. From their perspective, the husband's objections to his wife working outside the house must be surmounted so that social and economic benefits can be reaped. Nitza Ben Zvi of the Employment Service writes,

> The Ethiopian immigrant woman should be advanced and her status in the family strengthened. Her development will cause the whole family to develop, especially the children. . . . There is a need to disseminate information to convince women to go out to work and to help them understand the importance of going out. Information should also be given to the husbands.

No less naturally, social workers and others involved with Ethiopian families view domestic stability as their primary goal. Accordingly they point to the problems associated with the entry of women into the work force. From their perspective, the consequences of employment, not the fact of unemployment, lie at the heart of the matter. Beersheba community worker Naomi Arbel comments,

> It does cause some problems when the women are working because they find that working gives them a lot of strength and they have money that they can use for their own purposes and they want freedom and this causes a problem in the Ethiopian family. . . . Women that have money run counter to Ethiopian culture, because in Ethiopia the men handle all the economic matters in the family and not the women. . . . The economic force that the women acquire in Israel causes many women to decide to get a divorce.

Although it has often been suggested that the woman's decision to work outside the house is itself the cause of considerable tension and strife, this may be a case of the chicken and the egg. In some instances at least, women who view themselves as trapped in unsatisfactory marriages may seek outside work and the income it brings in order to gain independence. In such cases, the woman's work is not the problem, but (at least in her eyes) the solution. What is undeniable is the fact that in Israel a woman's options are far broader than they were in Ethiopia, and many take advantage of this, either within the framework of their marriages or outside it.

The tensions between women's traditional roles and the opportunities offered in Israel are most clearly seen when the wife goes out to work while the husband remains unemployed. Although the overall unemployment rate among Ethiopian women appears to be higher than among men, this situation is quite common. In Ethiopia, the husband was generally several years older than his wife. However, in some circumstances, second marriages for instance, he might be ten, twenty, even twenty-five years her senior. A 35 year-old woman will be offered more programs and probably adapt more quickly than her fifty-year-old husband. Indeed, at that age, unless he is part of the tiny minority of educated immigrants, he is unlikely to be seriously considered as a candidate for the work force. Once the wife is working, not only does her income make her more independent, but her exposure to the world around her greatly accelerates her adaptation. While she confronts the daily challenges of working life—Hebrew conversations, bus routes and schedules, work relations, pay slips, etc.—the husband remains behind, isolated, confused, frustrated.

Such a situation has implications for the family that extend beyond the relations between the couple themselves. While the Ethiopian woman's entry into the work force marks her exit from the domestic realm, she is *not* exchanging roles with her husband. Whatever her outside responsibilities, she is also expected to continue to perform all her household duties. Her husband will not assume them, and if she neglects them this is considered a major dereliction of her duty as a wife and mother. Often, in keeping with the traditional gender-based division of labor, much of the burden for running the household falls on the shoulders of an older daughter. She in turn must balance her duty to her parents as daughter with her responsibilities outside as a student. While her brothers are free to spend their afternoons doing homework or playing with friends, she may find herself confined to a daily routine of "woman's work."

30.4.6. Woman at work in the Ramat Gan diamond exchange, 1985.
(Doron Bachar, Beth Hatefutsoth.)

From "Old Virgins" to Singles and Soldiers

It is in the lives of girls and young women that the rift between traditional Ethiopian values regarding age and gender and Israeli norms can be most clearly seen. Ethiopian custom demanded that both as women and as children they live according to a restrictive code and defer to most of those around them. In Israel they are offered unparalleled freedom and opportunities. Only through a delicate balancing act can they both enjoy these benefits and maintain good relations with those more attached to customary norms.

In Ethiopia, girls were often engaged and even married by the time they reached puberty. If the girl was particularly young (some were as young as nine when they married), sexual relations were deferred until she was ready to bear children. Whatever her age, a girl was expected to be a virgin when she married. If it was discovered that she was not, the marriage would be annulled and she would be returned to her family. After she was married, the bride went to live in her husband's village with his family. She also became the responsibility of her husband, who was expected to support and protect her.

Marriages were arranged between families, not decided upon by the couple, who may never have met before their engagement had been announced. A match was agreed upon only after extended inquiries and negotiations conducted with the assistance of *qessotch* and *shmagilotch*. Traditionally, Beta Israel were forbidden to marry anyone from their *zamad,* as reckoned for seven generations. While this degree of separation between partners remained an ideal, in recent years as few as four generations has been accepted. In the course of reviewing genealogies for this purpose, the history of each family, its purity, and its standing were also investigated.

By the early 1970s, some Beta Israel girls in Ethiopia had begun to delay their marriages well past the age of puberty. Although relatively few in number, these "old virgins," as Michelle Schoenberger calls them ("old maid," although perhaps accurate, conjures up a totally wrong image for an unmarried 17–year-old!), challenged traditional categories concerning the age of marriage. They were, moreover, trendsetters for what was to follow in Israel.

The minimum legal age for marriage in Israel is sixteen. Although some ceremonies involving young girls were performed by Ethiopian *qessotch* in the mid-1980s, these were not sanctioned and had no legal standing. On the whole, Ethiopian girls in Israel do not marry before the completion of their high school studies at around the age of eighteen, and many wait considerably longer. They are not, however, necessarily "old virgins." Many, in fact, have been strongly influenced by the norms of their Israeli peers with regard to premarital relations.

At first, there was much confusion, and for some teenage girls, most of whom resided in boarding schools, the results were nothing short of a disaster. As Youth Aliyah anthropologist Anita Nudelman points out, such girls, who would have been wives and mothers in Ethiopia, had no real models for their behavior as singles and girl-friends and even less practical knowledge of birth control. Seeing their Israeli peers holding hands, hugging, and kissing in public (highly licentious behavior by Ethiopian standards), young immigrants understood this as evidence of the promiscuous norms of their new neighbors. They still retained, however, a fair degree of the Ethiopian woman's traditional deference to males. Pregnancies outside of marriage and in some cases abortions (both rare and strongly disapproved of in Ethiopia) followed.

In time, experience, education, and growing self-confidence paved the way for the development of a new pattern of premarital and marital relations. Couples date and even live together. Decisions to wed are made by individuals, but families are consulted and at least four generations of separation is usually observed. Couples who "discover" that they are more closely related usually agree to separate, although the decision is not an easy one. The expectation that the bride be a virgin is considered to be outmoded by many of the younger generation.

For many young women, the difficulty lies in balancing their desire to be part of the larger, more open society, and their continued respect

31.4.7. Teenage girls registering for Youth Aliyah, 1984. (Doron Bachar, Beth Hatefutsoth.)

for their parents. In a revealing interview with the *Jerusalem Post*, Tsega Melkav, a 24–year-old immigrant who divides her time between part-time studies at Bar Ilan University and work at Israel radio, spoke of sharing an apartment with her Ethiopian boyfriend:

> "My father is my father, we don't talk about it. . . . He knows we live together, but we don't talk about it. . . . If my father objects to my situation, there would be an argument, but it wouldn't change anything." Later, however, she adds almost wistfully, "There is a great deal of respect for the father in Ethiopia. . . . Now that my father is here [in Israel] I try to treat him like I did there. I don't want to hurt him; I want to try and preserve his honor."

Given the enthusiasm with which many Ethiopian women have embraced the freedoms and opportunities offered by Israeli society, it is perhaps a little surprising that so few have chosen to assume the major responsibility that that same society imposes upon its young people: compulsory military service. Unlike almost a thousand of their male counterparts, who have entered the Israeli armed forces and served, often with distinction, only about two dozen Ethiopian women have joined the Israeli Defense Forces. How can we explain this disparity?

On the most basic level, the answer is quite simple. Ethiopian women, in contrast to Ethiopian men, are not required to do military service, so most don't. This broad exemption appears to have its roots in both Ethiopian tradition and, perhaps more importantly, Israeli understanding of Ethiopian tradition.

In Israel, any woman can be excused from compulsory military service simply by claiming that she is religiously observant and that it would be difficult for her to maintain her "modesty" in the armed forces. Thousands of women are excused on this basis every year. Some volunteer to do alternative work in Sherut Le'umi (National Service) as teachers, hospital aides, etc. Others marry, study, and otherwise continue with their normal civilian lives.

Since Ethiopians are considered a traditionally religious community, their women are automatically exempted from military service. As we have already seen on several occasions, the reality of Ethiopian life in Israel is far more complex than the simple label "traditional"

32.4.8. President Chaim Herzog greets Ethiopian woman among a group of outstanding soldiers, Independence Day 1986. (Doron Bachar, Beth Hatefutsoth.)

indicates. Many of the changes we have discussed in this book, and particularly those that have taken place among young women, make a blanket characterization of Ethiopian women as "traditional" little short of absurd. Would the defense forces, for example, allow non-Ethiopian women who go to discotheques on Friday night to claim an exemption on religious grounds? One suspects not.

And yet, there seems to be little question that most Ethiopian parents do not want their daughters to go into the army, and that traditional beliefs play a part in this. Legends of warrior queens and the recent inclusion of women in the forces of various liberation movements notwithstanding, the army in Ethiopia (as in most countries) was perceived as a male realm par excellence. Women found in and around the army were almost exclusively in the lowly role of camp followers: prostitutes, washerwomen, beggars, etc. Ethiopian women came to Israel, therefore, with no tradition of martial values comparable to that of the men. In Israel, moreover, Ethiopians have, in the words of Shalva Weil, "a sense that women are loose in the army . . . so it takes time for the idea of women serving in the Israeli army to enter the consciousness of Ethiopian Jews."

More troubling, she notes, is the relatively low number, about two dozen, of Ethiopian women volunteering for Sherut Le'umi. Here, objections based on morality and tradition carry little weight. Rather, it appears that Ethiopian Jews are only slowly beginning to ask not what their country can do for them, but what they can do for their country.

We began this chapter by considering the encounter between Ethiopian men and female authority figures. We saw the manner in which the seemingly unbridgeable contradiction between "femaleness" and "power" was resolved by making absorption workers "honorary males." Other problems have proven more enduring. The changing status of women as they abandon traditional purity laws and forsake the domestic realm for the workplace has aggravated existing marital tensions and created new ones. Similarly, as the age of marriage for Ethiopian girls has risen, a new category of "singles" has emerged to challenge traditional assumptions and practices concerning premarital behavior and marriage. These complicated issues are not easily resolved, and the strains they produce will confront Ethiopian immigrants for many years. In the next chapter, we shall consider some of the ways they test Ethiopian families in Israel today.

CHAPTER FIVE

Families in Crisis

As the preceding chapters have demonstrated, the basic elements of traditional Ethiopian family life have been irreversibly transformed in the twentieth century. In the course of little more than a generation, both the internal dynamics and the external boundaries of the family have been radically redefined. Changes that began in imperial Ethiopia as part of a gradual evolutionary process gained momentum and accelerated in the wake of that country's revolution. A protracted and often traumatic *aliyah* process culminated in a wrenching encounter with Israeli norms of marital conduct, child rearing, and gender roles.

Not surprisingly, the "culture shock" experienced by Ethiopian immigrants both as individuals and as a society has been accompanied by a variety of disturbing phenomena. These include marital instability, domestic violence, and suicides. It is to these painful subjects that we turn our attention in this chapter.

Once again we must preface our discussion with a few words of explanation. The three topics we shall consider here are frequently cited as clear indications of the problems being experienced by Ethiopian Jews in Israel. There is much truth in this assertion, particularly in the case of suicides. The issues involved are, however, far more complex than a simple cause-effect relationship.

Despite the natural tendency of many Ethiopians to idealize family life in Ethiopia, divorce was common and the use of physical force

33.5.1. Elderly Ethiopian woman, Israel, 1991. (Bruce Bennett, JDC.)

was a familiar phenomenon. Since no statistics exist, it is, of course, impossible to say precisely how widespread they were and how much they have increased in Israel. What is certain and perhaps no less important is that here again the Ethiopians' move to Israel created a confrontation with new values and new conditions. Thus, the full significance of violent behavior within Ethiopian families in Israel can only be appreciated when it is understood that in many cases actions considered normal by Ethiopian standards are condemned as unacceptable in Israel. Similarly, while death, divorce, and separation may have produced many one-parent families in Ethiopia, the social and economic consequences of that status were radically different there from what they are in Israel. What existed in Ethiopia as one of many configurations in the organization of a household *(beta sa'ab)* becomes in Israel a symptom of marital crisis in a nuclear family.

Indeed, only in the case of suicides do we appear to be dealing with a comparatively "new" phenomenon among Ethiopians. Even in this case, however, it is difficult to draw a clear connection between these tragedies and any specific feature of absorption policy. The factors that play a part in these deaths are far more complex than has sometimes been claimed.

One-Parent Families: A New Problem or an Old Pattern?

No aspect of Ethiopian family life in Israel has aroused more comment among absorption workers and other professionals than the large number of one-parent families. Although no exact figures exist and household arrangements are in constant flux, in 1985 such families represented between 28 and 33 percent of all Ethiopian immigrants with children. (Among the general Israeli population, in comparison, only 8 percent of those families with children under the age of eighteen are single-parent families.) Among those who arrived in Operation Solomon, however, somewhere between a third and a half were in one-parent families! In Israel, as elsewhere, such families are overwhelmingly headed by women. Death, separation, and divorce have all played a role in the creation of this situation.

Here as elsewhere comparisons with Beta Israel society in Ethiopia are of only limited value. As Shalva Weil notes in her recent study of one-parent families, while "it appears that the frequency of divorcees, young widows, and abandoned women was high [in Ethiopia] . . . there is no recognized expression for one-parent families in Amharic or Tigrinya."

This is scarcely surprising. In the context of the Ethiopian household *(beta sa'ab)* and extended family *(zamad)* as described in chapter 3 above, the term "one-parent family" makes little sense. Children in a *beta sa'ab* were frequently not living with their biological parents. The death or absence of their father did not, moreover, usually place the children in a one-*adult* situation. Grandparents, older siblings, uncles, and aunts were usually close at hand. The safety net provided by the *zamad,* as well as a domestic economy that viewed children as an asset and put them to work at an early age, also cushioned any financial strain created by a particular member's absence.

This is not to say that such families did not suffer certain disadvantages. In particular, unattached women were vulnerable to sexual advances from a variety of men, including their ex-husbands. It does, however, raise serious questions as to whether there is any point in viewing what existed in Ethiopia as comparable to the one-parent family in Israel. Although the absence of one parent in both cases created a superficial resemblance between the two units, this was far outweighed by the larger cultural, social, and economic differences between them.

Many of the one-parent families found in Israel today were created, therefore, not by the *difficulties* associated with *aliyah,* but by the fact of *aliyah* itself. Placed in a new social-cultural context that emphasizes the nuclear family and is unaware of or ignores the *beta sa'ab* and *zamad,* they have acquired a new label, that of "one-parent family."

At the same time, many new one-parent families are being created. The reasons for this are many and varied, for as Tolstoy writes in *Anna Karenina,* "Happy families are all alike; every unhappy family is unhappy in its own way." In the case of Ethiopian immigrants they can, however, be grouped in several categories, many of which we have discussed above. Such families were created when couples made *aliyah* at different times, or when one of the partners died on the way to Israel. In Israel itself, the redefinition of gender roles, the abandonment of purity laws, conflicts over personal goals, and sharp differences between husbands and wives in their rates of adjustment to new conditions all contribute to the breakup of two-parent units. To these must also be added such "universal" factors as disagreements over child rearing (particularly acute in the new child-centered environment of Israel) and tensions created by crowded housing and low income.

In this context it must also be remembered that the move to Israel has both disrupted traditional forms of mediation conducted by *shamgilotch* and priests and added new "opportunities" for divorce. Thus, a woman dissatisfied with her situation in Ethiopia may have been convinced by a combination of social pressure and limited alternatives to remain with her husband. In Israel, the decline of the elders, her increased financial independence (either through a job or Social Security benefits), and the moral support of social workers all make divorce appear a more viable option.

Many elders and religious leaders clearly feel threatened by this new situation and mince no words in blaming Israeli insensitivity for much of the problem. Qes Imanu of Lod, an ebullient Ethiopian religious leader who is working through Betachin to revive traditional forms of mediation, comments,

> Now when there are conflicts between a couple and they go to the Israeli authorities, to a social worker, or to a lawyer they give them advice that is not always beneficial to them, because they don't understand the traditional Ethiopian way of life. Many times they escalate the conflict instead of resolving it and they take sides; especially the women. Usually the women are the ones who go and complain, and since the social workers are women, they automatically sympathize with the women. They don't understand the side of the men, of the husbands.

Alongside the forces described above that encourage the creation of new one-parent families among Ethiopian immigrants, it must also be remembered that other factors promote the creation of new house-

34.5.2. Mother and child moving into a new apartment, Netanya, 1985. (Doron Bachar, Beth Hatefutsoth.)

holds made up of members of earlier families. Single mothers find it difficult to both work and care for their children. Indeed, given the constraints of economic life in Israel, they find it difficult to make ends meet. For their part, men are not accustomed to performing domestic duties such as cooking and cleaning. While in Ethiopia it was comparatively easy to find a woman to perform such tasks, this is not always the case in Israel.

In Israel, therefore, Ethiopian couples encounter a variety of pressures that serve to both push them apart and pull them together. Family units form, separate, and reform with remarkable frequency. Once again, official statistics reveal only a fraction of the truth. Not all couples go through the formal processes of marriage and divorce. Others form households based on Ethiopian models that have no counterpart in Israeli officialdom.

Domestic Violence

Given the difficulties that face one-parent families in Israel, social workers and absorption officials are usually cautious in encouraging divorce unless all other options have been exhausted. One noticeable exception to this pattern appears in the cases of domestic violence. Confronted by a husband who beats his wife, Israeli officials usually act more quickly to separate the couple. Although a number of cases of extreme violence and even murder have led to accusations that the authorities respond too slowly, in the eyes of some Ethiopian men their behavior is often viewed as too hasty. As Qes Imanu comments, the (usually female) social workers say,

> "Why don't you go to the police and complain and go to a lawyer and fight for a divorce." When she [the Ethiopian woman] came, she didn't want to get divorced. She wanted to change her husband's behavior, but then she found a way to go for a divorce.

Few aspects of daily life more clearly divide cultures and societies than the amount and types of violence they find acceptable. Although the phrase "acceptable violence" may at first glance appear to be an

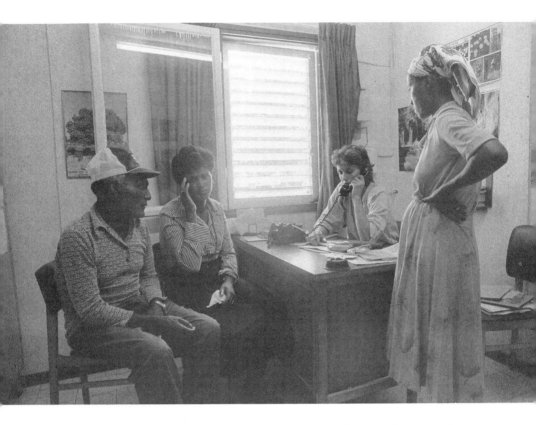

35.5.3. A family meeting with a social worker, Pardes Hannah, 1984.
(Doron Bachar, Beth Hatefutsoth.)

oxymoron, a self-contradictory phrase like "kind cruelty" or "make haste slowly," all societies view some forms of violence as "normal" while condemning others as intolerable. Many Muslims, for example, continue to permit "honor killings" when a woman has besmirched the family name, and "vengeance killings," when a family member has been murdered. For their part many Westerners view corporal punishment of children as permissible, but are appalled when some-one acts similarly toward a spouse, sibling, or parent.

When societies with sharply differing norms concerning violence are brought together, major misunderstandings and even tragedies can result. One such case concerning Ethiopians in Israel occurred at the outset of the Palestinian uprising known as the *intifada*. An Ethiopian soldier with a history of psychological problems killed a Palestinian shopkeeper who cursed him. It was difficult to tell who was more mystified by the case, the army legal corps, who couldn't understand why the Ethiopian had reacted so violently, or the soldier, who couldn't understand what he had done wrong. While the root cause of this tragedy was undoubtedly the soldiers' own deep emo-tional problems, which should have disqualified him from military service, cultural factors were also at play. As Dr. Chaim Rosen pointed out when consulted by the soldier's attorney, in the context of Ethio-pia's highly formalized etiquette and forms of address, to curse some-one is virtually equivalent to physical violence. While American chil-dren are taught to ignore verbal attacks ("Sticks and stones may break my bones . . ."), the Ethiopian proverbial wisdom is almost precisely the opposite: "The tongue has no bones, the tongue breaks bones!*

Although far less dramatic than this exceptional incident, eruptions of domestic violence are a much more common reminder of the gap that separates Ethiopian and Israeli norms on family behavior in general and on this subject in particular. At times even the most

---

* The tragic story of this one soldier is, fortunately, highly exceptional. Through careful preparation and innovative programming, the Israel armed forces have enjoyed tremen-dous success with Ethiopian recruits. Several hundred young Ethiopians have served in the various branches of the Israel Defense Forces, many in elite units and a number as officers.

experienced immigrants appear totally unaware of the impression they create. Thus, when addressing a symposium of educational psychologists in January of 1992, Akiva Baruch, a Betachin staff worker, spoke with remarkable frankness concerning this aspect of marital relations in Ethiopia. As his overwhelmingly female audience squirmed in discomfort, Akiva spoke of the "educational" function served when a husband disciplined his wife. Using language that many Israelis (although perhaps not psychologists) would have readily accepted if applied to parent-child relations, he spoke of the need to "correct" misbehavior, to return the wife to the correct path, to act promptly to prevent more serious difficulties in the future. In short: spare the rod, spoil the wife.

In fact, corporal punishment appears to have been a fairly normal part of marital relations in Ethiopia and to have followed any significant failure of the wife to fulfill her duties. Wife beating in the sense of excessive violence (and once again the term "excessive" is culturally determined) does not appear to have been particularly common. If repeated, it was grounds for divorce. Nevertheless, the overall level of domestic violence was probably high by Western standards.

Domestic violence by Ethiopians in Israel appears to be shaped by at least two separate factors. First, the difference between Ethiopian norms and that of the dominant society has led to a clear perception that violent behavior is a problem within Ethiopian families. In other words, behavior that in Ethiopia might have been viewed as acceptable is labeled in Israel as problematic and even illegal. In this context, it is worth noting that many Israelis' own sensitivity to domestic violence is of fairly recent origin. Condemning the phenomenon among the Ethiopian immigrants is one way of highlighting their own newly acquired awareness. Certainly, there has been a dramatic rise in the amount of coverage devoted to domestic violence by the Israeli media and society at large in recent years. In some senses, therefore, the Ethiopians' behavior is caught in the spotlight of this newfound concern.

Second, domestic violence is probably more common in Israel than it was in Ethiopia. Given the lack of statistics on this subject from Ethiopia we can, of course, only speculate. Increased violence is a phenomenon that has been commented upon among a variety of refugee groups and its existence among Ethiopians in Israel would not, therefore, be surprising. More specifically, the changes and tensions that have confronted Ethiopian families in Israel would appear to be a fertile breeding ground for "corrective" violence of the sort explained by Akiva Baruch and for even more severe incidents that end in serious injury or death. As women increasingly assert themselves and explore the new opportunities they are offered, men make use of all the means at their disposal in an attempt to keep them in line. Since family and communal pressures are far less effective than in Ethiopia, violence becomes a more common means of achieving this goal.

Suicides

The violence that plagues Ethiopian families in Israel is not limited to acts directed against others. Since the period of Operation Moses it is estimated that more than sixty Ethiopians (about five times the rate for other Israelis) have taken their lives while living in Israel.

Under the best of circumstances it is difficult to unequivocally state the reason why a particular person commits suicide while another in similar circumstances does not. In the case of Ethiopian immigrants in Israel the problem is complicated by both a lack of firm statistics and recurrent attempts to politicize the phenomenon. Because of the latter, painful personal and family tragedies are exploited to score points in ongoing political debates. Thus, during the conflict with the Rabbinate, suicides were said to have resulted from the inability of Ethiopians to marry legally, but in discussions concerning university studies the same cases were claimed to have followed refusal of admission to the university. While the suicides following Operation Moses were often attributed to the trauma of *aliyah,* the guilt of "survivors' syndrome," and concern for relatives in Ethiopia, the massive family reunification of Operation Solomon, far from putting an end to such tragedies, produced a new wave of deaths. Most recently, in an editorial published on December 20, 1991, *The Jeru-*

salem Post argued (apparently on the basis of a single case) that Ethiopian suicides in Israel were not connected to difficulties in the absorption process, but were directly attributable to the failure to bring the *faras moura*, Beta Israel who had converted to Christianity, to Israel.

The attempts of the *Post* and others notwithstanding, any attempt to find a single cause and a simple solution to the problem of Ethiopian suicides in Israel appears doomed to failure. Unlike domestic violence and divorce, suicide does not appear to have been common among the Beta Israel in Ethiopia. This does not mean, however, that it is the result of any one feature of their experience in Israel. Even if we exclude for the moment the devastating impact of the *aliyah* process itself, no simple answers appear. Reports concerning Ethiopian refugees in the United States, Germany, Canada, and resettlement camps in Ethiopia itself all mention a disturbingly high rate of suicides. Given the vast differences that separate these countries and their refugee programs, it seems unlikely that a common denominator will be found on this level. This does not mean, of course, that we can abandon the attempt to understand and, most importantly, prevent such occurrences. It does, however, warn us to be skeptical of anyone offering a simple solution for so complex a problem.

A look at a few of the suicides that have occurred since Operation Moses seems to support the link between at least some of these incidents and the kind of absorption difficulties we have discussed above. On December 14, 1991, for example, a Christian Ethiopian who feared he would be returned to Ethiopia if his Beta Israel wife carried out her threat to divorce him murdered her and then committed suicide. Later the same month, an Ethiopian Jew engaged in a violent quarrel with his wife struck her, knocking her unconscious. Fearing that he had killed her, the man himself committed suicide. Other cases earlier the same year included a father of eight, who killed himself following an extended period of unemployment, and another whose suicide appears to have been connected to having tested positive for AIDS.

The manner in which a series of misfortunes can culminate in disaster is illustrated by the case of a young Ethiopian mother of three

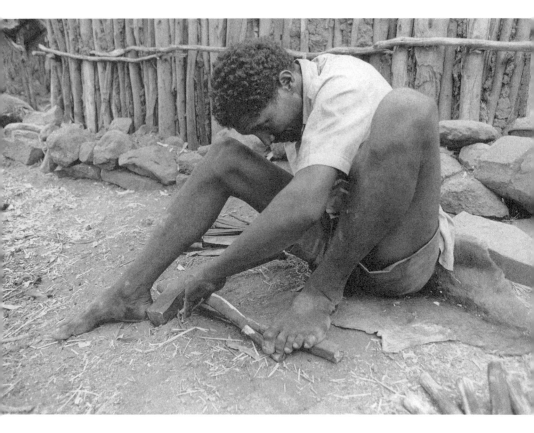

36.5.4. Asayan Negate working as a blacksmith in Ethiopia, Passover 1984. He later made *aliyah* and settled with his family in Ashqelon. In 1991, he committed suicide. (Doron Bachar, Beth Hatefutsoth.)

living in Netanya, who committed suicide in February 1992. Abandoned by her husband, who had beaten her, deeply in debt, separated by many miles from her parents, who lived in Beersheva, and unable or unwilling to make use of the local mental health services, she hanged herself in despair.

One theme that surfaces in many of these cases is the feeling of being trapped and powerless that appears to have affected the victims. Unable to live in honorable fashion in a country whose rules and customs remain unfamiliar, the Ethiopian seeks to exert at least a measure of control by dying with honor. In contrast to the usual norm, in which attempted suicides outnumber deaths by nearly ten to one, among Ethiopians the proportion narrows to two or three to one. Put bluntly, when Ethiopians attempt suicide they are not making a call for help; they are trying to kill themselves—to die with their honor intact.

As Chaim Rosen points out, it is this loss of hope (the Amharic term for despair or depression, *tesfa maqwrat*, means literally "the cutting off of hope") that may hold the key to understanding the plight of many of these victims. No matter how difficult conditions were in Ethiopia, how desperate their circumstances in the Sudan, or how trying the wait in Addis Ababa, the Beta Israel could always hold on to their hope of reaching Zion. For many of them, Israel was a magical land where anything was possible. Some even believed that people did not die in the land of Israel. Ironically, the fulfillment of their dream of coming to Israel has denied them the kind of hope that often served as a last wall of defense against despair. To be in dire straits after making *aliyah* is all the more excruciating, because one could no longer hope for deliverance through coming to the Promised Land. Not surprisingly, in light of this suggestion, the teen suicides found in many Western countries are comparatively rare among the Ethiopians. It is the older generation and, for reasons we have outlined above, particularly men, who are most vulnerable to this loss of hope and honor. For one group of Ethiopians at least, survival may have been made more difficult by salvation.

Finally, it must be remembered that suicides are both a symptom of difficulties and a cause of difficulties. Often our desire to understand the circumstances that have led the victim to take his or her life blinds us to the tragedy of the survivors: children, spouses, parents, and siblings. Viewed from the perspective of the family, suicide is like a stone thrown into a pond, producing both a large splash and a series of waves. In its wake it leaves behind orphans, widows and widowers, one-parent families, and bereaved elders. It produces yet one more chink in the fragile structure of Ethiopian family life.

The transformation of the Ethiopian family in Israel has been accompanied by a number of troubling phenomena, including divorce, domestic violence, and suicide. As we have seen in this chapter, it would be a tremendous oversimplification to say that any of these are "caused" by immigration to Israel. At least in part, one-parent families are a continuation of a traditional form of Beta Israel social organization. *Aliyah*, however, redraws the boundaries of the family and replaces the large and complex *beta sa'ab* with the smaller nuclear family. The absence or death of one of the parents thus acquires a new significance. Similarly, much of the domestic violence found among Ethiopian Jews in Israel originates in patterns of behavior viewed as acceptable in their country of origin. In Israel the redefinition of norms of conduct within the family makes the continuation of such actions a social and legal problem.

The troubles confronting Ethiopians in Israel cannot, however, be simply reduced to a shift in cultural codes. Although no precise statistics exist, compared to Ethiopia, families in Israel appear less stable, domestic violence more common, and suicide more frequent. In part, these increases can be attributed to the rapid changes being experienced and to the tensions produced in their aftermath. The decline of traditional forms of mediation, social pressure, and communal support have all also played a part.

CHAPTER SIX

People and Programs

Thus far we have attempted to describe some of the challenges facing Ethiopian immigrants in Israel. We have chronicled the difficulties they confront in a variety of spheres, including housing, religion, parent-child relations, and changing gender roles. We have seen the dramatic impact of recent changes in Ethiopia, of a dramatic and traumatic *aliyah,* and especially of the absorption process in Israel. Throughout all of our discussions two themes have recurred with remarkable regularity. First, we have returned repeatedly to differences between the culture that the Ethiopians left behind and that which they have encountered in Israel. Second, we have seen that almost all the changes undergone by Ethiopian immigrants to Israel have a direct effect on the stability and function of their families.

The picture that we have drawn thus far has been one-sided and perhaps unduly pessimistic. While we have discussed the problems in some detail, except for a few references to the work done by the Betachin family counseling service, we have yet to consider the attempts that have been made to solve them. These are the subject of this, our final chapter. Here we shall focus on some of the people and programs that are attempting to ease the Ethiopians' adjustment to their new surroundings.

Before we begin to discuss specific examples, a few words of explanation are in order. In selecting these cases, it has not been our intention to slight or downplay the importance of other similar efforts that are not mentioned in this book. The programs considered below represent only a fraction of those currently operating and have been chosen first and foremost for their relevance to our themes of culture and the family. Thus, important programs in teacher training, Hebrew instruction, and vocational education have not been included.

We have also limited ourselves in this chapter to the discussion of relatively small programs with clearly defined targets. As a result we shall have little to say about the large-scale efforts of the organizations that have invested the most time, energy, and resources to the absorption process: the Jewish Agency, the Ministry of Immigrant Absorption, and the Ministry of Labor and Social Affairs. It is impossible to do justice to programs of such magnitude in the limited space at our disposal. Indeed, to consider their work with the Ethiopians without describing their efforts to simultaneously absorb more than ten times as many immigrants from the former Soviet Union would be to do them a grave injustice. One merely needs to remember that the four hundred thousand immigrants brought to Israel over the past two years is the equivalent proportionately of the United States accepting twenty-five million!

Guarding a Legacy

Long before most Jews had even heard of the Beta Israel, Israel's second president Itzhak Ben Zvi, had begun to devote his attention to this enigmatic "lost tribe." Over the years, he regularly expressed concern for their welfare and encouraged activities on their behalf. When the first Ethiopian children were brought to Israel in the 1950s, the president took a special interest in them and met with them on several occasions. Yosef David, one of those children and today a counselor at Betachin, remembers those days fondly: "President Ben Zvi was the father of Ethiopian Jewry. He saw us like his children, he hosted us and let us use his library. He said we were true Jews." In

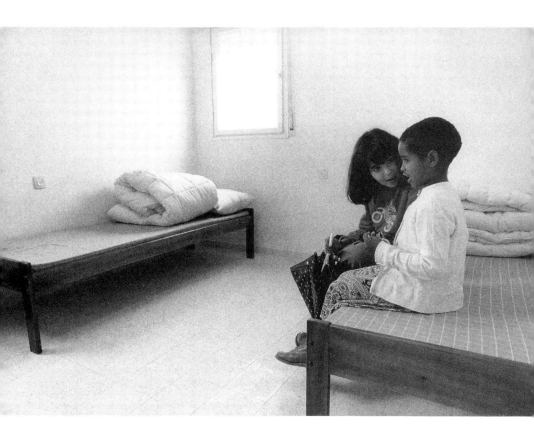

37.6.1. Meeting a neighbor on the first day in permanent housing,
Nazareth Ilit, 1985. (Doron Bachar, Beth Hatefutsoth.)

remembrance of his kindness, Yosef named his first son Ben Zvi. As a more general token of its appreciation, the community presented the President with a copy of the Orit (Ge'ez Bible), their most sacred book.

Given Ben Zvi's concern for the Jews of Ethiopia, it was only fitting that the institute that bears his name was selected by the Jewish Agency to take the lead in the study and documentation of Beta Israel culture. In 1983 the Ben Zvi Institute for the Study of Jewish Communities in the East inaugurated a project designed to record and study the history and culture of the Jews of Ethiopia. At the time of Operation Moses, it was the only academic institution in Israel with an ongoing program on Ethiopian Jewry.

A major portion of the institute's project is devoted to working alongside Ethiopian Jews to protect their unique cultural heritage. While such work is of importance in the case of any traditional society undergoing the trauma of resettlement, in the case of Ethiopian Jews it has a special urgency. Although the Beta Israel do have a small number of sacred texts, theirs was in the main an oral culture. Crucial communal values and traditions were transmitted from generation to generation by word of mouth or through rituals.

The move to Israel, the decline of the *shmagilotch* and *qessotch*, the "normalization" of religious practice to conform more closely to rabbinic Judaism, and the transfer of children's education from the family to the schools have all put this chain of transmission in danger. Moreover, since most traditional knowledge has never been written down, the death of an elder or priest is equivalent to the destruction of an entire library. Knowledge lost today can never be retrieved.

In recognition of this special situation, the Ben Zvi Institute has devoted much of its energy to documenting and preserving the oral heritage of Ethiopian Jewry. Cooperating with a variety of institutions, including the Israeli National Music Archives, the Diaspora Museum in Tel Aviv, and the Institute for Contemporary Jewry at Hebrew University, Ben Zvi researchers seek to guard oral traditions of Ethiopian Jewry as a legacy for future generations.

From the outset this work has been conceived of as a partnership between the institute and the Ethiopian community. While the partic-

38.6.2. Qes Ameha Negat Tafeta at the Ben Zvi Institute reading an *Orit* (Torah) that once belonged to his father and was given as a gift to Itzhak Ben Zvi. (Shimon Rubenstein, Ben Zvi Institute.)

ipation of Ethiopian immigrants has, of course, always been essential to the project, their role has changed over time. At first, they were involved exclusively as informants and translators. In the early 1980s and in the period immediately after Operation Moses, most immigrants were far more concerned with the daily demands of their new society than with recording and documenting the old. Researchers' inquiries were often met with suspicion, which only gradually changed to pleasure that someone was interested in their history and traditions. Even when the project and a number of its researchers became familiar to the Ethiopian community, the control and definition of the project remained almost exclusively in the hands of non-Ethiopians.

In more recent years, the Ethiopians' role in documenting their culture has grown. A small number of immigrants, having successfully overcome the first hurdles in their integration into Israeli society, have begun to turn their attention to the world they left behind. More and more, they not only define the areas to be studied, but conduct the research as well. In such cases, the personal quest for roots and the desire to serve the community by documenting its past are often almost indistinguishable. Belaynish Zevadiah, a Hebrew University graduate student, is collecting oral histories about the pre-*aliyah* contacts between Ethiopian Jews and Israelis. Her eventual goal is a thesis on the life of her late father, one of the community's foremost religious authorities and most respected leaders. Hers will undoubtedly be only the first of many attempts by Ethiopian Jews to capture the wisdom of the older generation for their descendants and tell ancient stories in a new language.

Translating Culture

Sooner or later everyone who works with Ethiopian Jews in Israel is referred to Dr. Chaim Rosen. If they're lucky, it's sooner rather than later. American born and educated, Rosen spent four years in Ethiopia with the Peace Corps and collecting data for his University of Chicago doctorate. He is therefore the only person in Israel who brings both academic training and first-hand experience in Ethiopia to his work with Ethiopian Jews. Soft-spoken and unassuming, Rosen eschews politics and bureaucratic infighting in order to reach as many people as possible. Although officially employed by the Ministry of Immigrant Absorption, he makes his expertise available to anyone who works with Ethiopians.

Rosen's message is essentially a simple one: Only by learning the categories and terms that Ethiopian Jews use to understand the world can we begin to make sense of their behavior in Israel. Only through an appreciation of how *they* believe a child should be raised, a youth should behave, and an adult must act will we be able to comprehend the conflicts they face and work with them toward solutions.

Under the sponsorship of Hadassah Women's Council, Rosen has developed and disseminated his ideas in a series of papers and articles. He rapidly became the Dear Abby (or should we say the Dr. Ruth?) of those working with Ethiopian immigrants, answering questions on almost every aspect of Ethiopian life: What's the best way to phrase an invitation? Why do they seem to have so many names? Why do they accept apartments in one city, but not in another?

Throughout his writings and lectures Rosen explores the manner in which key elements of Beta Israel culture can be applied to the design and implemention of successful absorption programs. Understanding Ethiopian culture does not require us to either idealize it or artificially preserve it. It does, however, demand both careful study and imaginative application of old concepts to new situations.

Rosen notes, for example, the centrality of the Amharic concept *gobez*. "Smart, brilliant, clever, strong, brave, and, finally, quite a fellow. Every Ethiopian boy (and in her own way, girl) desires more than anything else to be considered *gobez*." In Ethiopia, someone who was *gobez* might beat an opponent in battle, endure a long fast, show great skill and determination at a difficult job. People had to be *gobez* to survive their long trek to the Sudan and the many hardships they encountered.

The trick is, of course, to translate this central value into a meaningful part of Ethiopian life in Israel: to make it *gobez* to learn well in school, to serve with honor in the army, to act in a way that benefits yourself, your family, and your community. Not without reason did

Rosen entitle an information booklet about sexually transmitted diseases prepared in cooperation with Dr. Daniel Chemtov of Hebrew University-Hadassah Medical School, *Be "Gobez" to Stay Healthy*. In it they write, "As the *gobez* farmer in Ethiopia will stop monkeys and baboons [from attacking his crops] by building a strong fence and being a good shot, so the *gobez* individual in Israel (both man and woman) will know when and how to use a condom."

In some cases, the information provided by Rosen has been the catalyst for major changes in programs involving Ethiopian Jews. Following Operation Moses, for example, a course was established at the Hebrew University-Hadassah Medical School to train Ethiopian women as dental assistants. Almost from the outset the course was in trouble, as the Ethiopian students struggled to master the theoretical background necessary for their practical training. Some instructors estimated that the course might have to be extended to three times its normal length for them to complete it. Even then their success was in doubt.

During the search for answers, the director of the course, Dr. Yonatan Mann, met with Chaim Rosen, who explained the importance of the Amharic term *tabib*. Although translated literally as "wisdom," *tabib*, like its equivalent in Biblical Hebrew, *hochma*, refers to both intellectual erudition and practical skill. In Ethiopia the Beta Israel were often proficient craftsmen. As such they were frequently derided as *tabiban* by their neighbors, who envied and even feared their "wizardry" with their hands. Many Beta Israel, however, took great pride in their skill as blacksmiths, weavers, and potters. Rosen also explained the "hands-on" approach that characterized traditional education in Ethiopia. When a woman wished to teach her daughter to make pots, she didn't sit her down for a lecture on the history of clay or the theory of pottery. Rather, she gave her different types of clay and water, and taught by example, through a slow process of trial and error.

Dr. Mann decided to gamble and follow the "traditional" method. Theoretical classes were deferred to the end of the course, and the students were moved immediately into the practical side. Results improved almost immediately as the Ethiopian women quickly grasped the mechanical side of their new professions. Moreover, when they moved back into the classroom to complete the material that had been deferred, their progress was much easier. In the end, with only a minimal extension of the course, the majority of Ethiopian students completed it successfully. Most began to work at their new professions, and some continued their studies in the more advanced dental hygienist course.

Serving by Example

While many young Ethiopians have discovered how to handle their own affairs, for the elderly, and all others who have not learned to speak Hebrew well, it is vital to find someone to serve as a mediator. Some turn to veteran immigrants—especially relatives. Others develop a special friendship with a sympathetic Israeli who is willing to intervene and assist in areas such as home repairs, court cases, job interviews, and wedding arrangements.

Another option is to call upon one of the Ethiopians who has graduated from a two-year course at Netanya, organized by the Ministry of Labor and Social Affairs, the Ministry of Immigrant Absorption, and Amishav, the Joint Distribution Committee's Center for Aid to Ethiopian Immigrants. According to their credentials upon graduation they are "educational-social workers," and none has the formal training required to be either a regular social or community worker. (About half the Netanya graduates are, however, today studying to become social workers.) Generally, these graduates help municipal social workers in dealing with the needs of Ethiopians who have left absorption centers for permanent apartments. More than anyone else the Netanya graduates have begun to serve their community as effective advocates.

During 1989, for example, two such Ethiopian workers in the Israeli port city of Ashdod handled 560 applications requiring their intervention with various organizations and agencies. These included securing household appliances (ovens, refrigerators, etc.) from the Ministry of Absorption, reductions in municipal taxes or water rates from the city, apartment repairs from Amigur (the housing authority), and various services (child allowances, disability payments, unemployment benefits) from the Social Security Office.

In addition to representing the interests of Ethiopians at the various offices, these community workers have taken the initiative throughout the country in confronting a number of other problem areas. Their efforts have included setting up an after-school center for Ethiopian children, helping organize parents' groups through which Ethiopian parents are taught to understand and participate in their children's education, and arranging for community centers to offer handicraft classes and Hebrew lessons to the elderly.

As much as the community workers attempt to handle people's affairs on a daily basis, they also try to encourage those they help to take initiative. In this manner they hope to wean them from the helplessness and dependency that so many Ethiopian immigrants develop. These efforts at fostering self-sufficiency are in the long run an even more important contribution to their clients' welfare than the immediate solutions they provide by direct intervention.

Avraham Yissaskhar, a community worker in Ramla, south of Tel Aviv, not only assists Ethiopian immigrants in locating plumbers and repair persons, but also has made it possible for them to do much of this work themselves. At his initiative a home maintenance course was set up for Ethiopian immigrants. "My clients didn't know how to deal with a leaky faucet. They didn't know how to unplug a drain. . . . I developed the [home maintenance] program with the social services bureau. At the end of the course, each participant received a toolbox."

While most people who approach the community workers expect them to be able to solve their problems, or to be able to obtain things they require, some come only to ask for advice and encouragement. Batya, a widow with seven children, came to ask Shmuel Meheret, an Ashdod worker, for assistance in receiving a rent reduction because of her family situation. Shmuel told her that she could write a letter, but was skeptical since she had already received one such reduction. She told him, "I'll go anyway; it can't hurt to ask." She requested instructions, but insisted on going by herself. Shmuel is lavish in his

39.6.3. Nursery school teacher celebrates the Jewish New Year with her students, Jerusalem. (JDC.)

praise of her "brave, manly [!] spirit." He is obviously proud of her for taking the initiative and using him only for what she is not *yet* able to do alone.

What this case and the home maintenance course both suggest is that the Ethiopians who will function best in Israel are those who only rely on outside help until they can handle their own affairs. At the same time as they value the assistance they receive from their community workers today, they also see them as models and try to cultivate such abilities in themselves and in their children.

Building a Community

Of the many programs attempting to service and assist Ethiopian families in Israel, the Community and Education Project for Beta Israel that operates in the city of Beersheva is certainly one of the most ambitious and successful. Known popularly as the "Van Leer Project" because it was supported by the Bernard Van Leer Foundation for several years, it has developed a uniquely broad range of programs that extend from infancy to old age.

In contrast to the Netanya-trained Ethiopian community workers, who serve as resources for entire communities, the Beersheva project involves a far broader range of contacts with the immigrant population. The Beersheva Ethiopian community, which even before Operation Solomon numbered over two thousand immigrants, is one of the largest in the country. Through patient and painstaking work the project organizers have avoided the pitfalls of politicization and paternalism and have succeeded in forging links throughout much of the city's Ethiopian population. From its inception the project has been based on the assumption that its success would be measured by its ability to work with, rather than for, the Ethiopian community. The first step in this process was the decision to establish the project office and meeting rooms in the heart of a predominantly Ethiopian neighborhood. This was immediately followed by a series of training programs designed to involve Ethiopians in both the day-to-day running and the long-range planning of the project. Through courses funded with Amishav, a number of Ethiopian women were trained as childcare workers. Mothers of young children were encouraged to pursue in-service training toward becoming paraprofessionals in childcare and early childhood education. They in turn became advocates for the program among their neighbors, friends, and extended families. Unlike many programs that have token Ethiopian representation, seven of the fifteen members of the project's steering committee are drawn from the local immigrant community. Indeed, almost all the project's programs involve Ethiopians working to help Ethiopians.

While the Ethiopian families in Beersheva have many of the same problems found throughout the country, community worker Naomi Arbel singles out one for special mention. Her concern rests with the first generation of Ethiopian Jews born in Israel:

> The children who are born in Israel seem to be lost, because they don't have the values that they had in Ethiopia. . . . We have many problems with these children, behavior problems that you don't find among those children who came at the age of ten or eleven . . . and came with all the good habits and traditions of Ethiopia.

Many of the project's programs are designed precisely to deal with this issue. Thus a cooperative preschool brings together eighty Ethiopian and non-Ethiopian children from age fourteen months to three years. Two paraprofessional women work with each group of twenty children, and every mother takes a turn assisting in her child's group. Once a week, mothers are invited to "coffee hour" discussions with project staff and other experts. By working with the Ethiopian families rather than entrusting the children to non-Ethiopian caretakers, the program maintains the crucial link between parent and child. In addition, non-Ethiopian children receive the benefit of a positive encounter with their new neighbors.

An even larger number of families are part of a home visit program in which paraprofessionals meet with mothers of children from infancy to age three. Although the program was initially designed with mother-child relations as its primary target, the contacts established through it have been crucial in establishing the credibility of the project throughout the community. Staff members' reputations for sensitivity and discretion quickly led to their visits being treated as an opportunity to raise a variety of issues concerning childraising and marital relations.

In keeping with its commitment to take the community's needs as its starting point for all programs, the project has remained dynamic and has continued to evolve. In response to a lack of afternoon care for young children, a latchkey program was developed. Today, eighty children, four to seven years old, participate in an after-school program in which they receive a hot meal, rest, any help they need with their homework, and various enrichment programs.

The arrival in the community of older children who had spent their first years in Israel in Youth Aliyah boarding schools has produced leadership programs and courses in preparing for university matriculation exams. Other activies include a big brother/big sister program and a grandparent-grandchild group in which both generations share handicrafts and other activities. The last of these serves not only the Ethiopian youngsters, but also the elders, "many of whom just sit at home and get social security money and don't do anything special."

It is doubtful if any single component of the Beersheva project is in itself unique. Throughout Israel different agencies are running similar programs. What is most noteworthy here is the comprehensiveness of the project. By combining the programs described above with others, including health education, teen clubs, parent groups, and others, the Beersheva project is doing nothing less than creating a new locally-based community. Nothing can replace the social networks that dissolved when the immigrants left Ethiopia, but the Beersheva project goes a long way toward creating a new support system. In the words of Project Director Chasia Levin,

> Just as a single stone tossed into a still pool of water causes ever-widening wavelets circling out into infinity, so our work, activated by the simple act of reaching out to the first bewildered child and mother, has resulted in ever-widening circles of involvement and acceptance.

Despite their differences, all the people and programs discussed in this chapter can be said to have several crucial features in common. First, all four rely on a familiarity with traditional Ethiopian culture. While this is most obvious in the documentation work of the Ben Zvi Institute and the applied anthropology of Chaim Rosen, it applies no less to the other two projects. In Beersheva, for example, the Ethio-

40.6.4. Big brother and sister tutoring program, Beersheba, 1991. (JDC.)

pian paraprofessionals both explain Ethiopian behavior and customs to outsiders and encourage Ethiopian mothers "to utilize their experience and heritage from Ethiopia in rearing their children [in Israel]." Even the use of the Netanya-trained community workers to assist in contacts with government institutions is based, perhaps unconsciously, on the widespread use of mediators in Ethiopian political culture.

Second, although designed by non-Ethiopians, each program carries within it the seeds of an increasing Ethiopian involvement that will eventually culminate in either its obsolescence or its complete restructuring. When a cadre of Ethiopian researchers has been trained there will be little need for outside initiatives of the type pursued by Chaim Rosen or at the Ben Zvi Institute. Already a growing number of Ethiopian immigrants are working as teachers and social workers serving not only their own community but also the general population.

The goal of the Ethiopian community workers is not, therefore, to achieve permanent employment as representatives of a marginalized and dependent clientele, but to serve as the bridge through which more and more immigrants will obtain confidence and competence in their daily lives. For this, if for no other reason, many are preparing for the future by training as social workers qualified to serve all Israelis.

In the same manner, the Beersheva project seeks not to preserve the Ethiopians as an isolated subculture, but to provide them with the tools for claiming their proper place within the larger Israeli society. For the present it seeks to work with the local immigrant population and to serve as a model for other similar projects. Its true success will be seen only when Israelis of Ethiopian heritage (no longer mere immigrants) have no greater need for special programs than any other group in the country. Indeed, this will in the final analysis be the one true indication of their successful integration into Israeli society.

During the 1980s the center of Beta Israel life shifted from Ethiopia to Israel. In the 1990s Ethiopian Jewry as an active and living Diaspora community came to an end. In late summer 1992, the last group

41.6.5. Ethiopian immigrant in original clothes, Ashqelon, 1984.
(Doron Bachar, Beth Hatefutsoth.)

42.6.6. The same boy with new clothes, Ashqelon, 1984. (Doron Bachar, Beth Hatefutsoth.)

flight of Jews from Ethiopia arrived in Israel. The remaining Beta Israel, estimated at 300, are being brought individually, with all due in Israel by the winter of 1992. Thus, in a period of little over fifteen years, from 1977 to 1992, an entire community will have been transported from one civilization to another. Seldom in human history has so complete a transformation occurred in so short a period.

When the remaining Beta Israel arrive in Israel, they will join over forty thousand of their fellow Ethiopians who made the journey before them. In addition to a new language, strange foods, and unfamiliar cultural norms, they will also encounter over seven thousand Israeli-born Ethiopian Jews, who had never been in Ethiopia. In this book, we have attempted to tell the story of both generations: the last Beta Israel born in Ethiopia, and the first Ethiopian Jews born in Israel.

As we noted in our introduction, much of the story we have told is captured in the pictures that grace our cover. The elegant white dresses and embroidered *shammas* (shawls) of Ethiopia are preserved in plastic bags, but as daily wear they have been replaced by Western jackets, jeans, and sneakers. More importantly, parents (front and center in the first picture) have been pushed into the background. A new generation with neither a firm grasp of the past nor a clear vision of the future has assumed center stage.

Much of what the Beta Israel encounter in Israel is the common lot of all immigrants and refugees. Changes in diet, clothing, housing, language, and economic status are only a few of the "normal" challenges they face in their new home. All of these, however, are filtered through the specific lenses of Ethiopian culture and society. Their saga is, therefore, both universal and unique.

Inevitably the story we have told remains incomplete. Since more than half of the Ethiopian Jews have been in Israel less than two years, it is far too early to offer a definitive answer to the Ed Koch-like question, "How are they doing?" In this book we have therefore not attempted to provide a single final answer, but new information and fresh insights. As both of us know from our own experience as immigrants, resettlement is a process that takes years rather than months, and at some levels is never truly complete. When Ethiopian Jews descend from the planes that bring them to Israel, their journey has not ended; it has only begun. Only time will tell whether their dramatic salvation from the chaos enveloping their ancient homeland will be followed by their survival as a dynamic and thriving people in their new home.

Glossary

aliyah, pl. *aliyot:* [Heb.] Immigration to Israel

amachenat: [Amh.] Relatives by marriage

Amishav: Center for Aid to Ethiopian Immigrants; part of the JDC

ashkar: [Amh.] literally servant; term of address for a young boy

baaltet: [Amh.] Elderly women

beta sa'ab: [Amh.] Household

buda: [Amh.] Evil-eye

Ethiopic: Ge'ez

faras mura or *falas mura:* [Amh.] Beta Israel converts to Christianity

Ge'ez: Classical Ethiopic; scriptural and liturgical language of Ethiopian Christians and Beta Israel

halacha: [Heb.] Rabbinic law

JDC: Joint Distribution Committee, American-based Jewish philanthropic organization active throughout the world, including Israel and Ethiopia

Jewish Agency: See *Sochnut Ha-yehudit*

ma'abarot: [Heb.] Transit camps that housed Israeli immigrants in the 1950s

mamzer: [Heb.] Illegitimate child; a child born of parents forbidden to engage in sexual relations with each other

mikve: [Heb.] Jewish ritual bath

mohel: [Heb.] Ritual circumcisor

niddah: [Heb.] Jewish laws of menstrual purity that dictate that a

139

women may not engage in sexual relations during the period of her menses and for seven days after, a minimum of twelve days

oleh, fem. *olah,* pl. *olim, olot:* [Heb.] Immigrant(s)

Orit: Ge'ez translation of the Bible, sometimes also used to refer to only the first five books

Qes, pl. *qessotch:* [Amh.] Priest

shmagile, pl. *shmagilotch:* [Amh.] Elder

Sochnut Ha-yehudit: The Jewish Agency, a nongovernmental organization responsible for bringing immigrants to Israel and caring for them during their first year in the country

tallithot: [Heb.] Prayer shawl

teffilin: [Heb.] Phylacteries

ulpan: [Heb.] Hebrew language schools

vatiq, pl. *vatiqim:* [Heb.] Veterans, old-timers in contrast to new immigrants

yadem gojo: [Amh.] Literally, hut of blood; menstrual hut

yamargam gojo: [Amh.] Literally, hut of the curse, menstrual hut

yaras gojo: [Amh.] Literally, hut of the woman in childbed; hut where mother and newborn wait in isolation for eighty days for a girl and forty days for a boy

yesaga zamad: [Amh.] Literally, family of the flesh; blood relations as opposed to relatives by marriage, *amachenat*

zamad: [Amh.] Extended family, often counted back over seven generations

Selected Bibliography

Abbink, G. Jan. *The Falashas in Ethiopia and Israel: The Problem of Ethnic Assimilation.* Nijmegen: Sociaal Antropolische Cahiers 15, 1984.

Ashkenazi, Michael, and Alex Weingrad. *Ethiopian Jews and Israel.* New Brunswick, N.J.: Transaction Books, 1987.

Ben-Ezer, Gadi, and Haim Peri. *Displaced Children: A Report of the Condition of Displaced Jewish Children in Addis Ababa.* Jerusalem: Israel Section of Defence for Children International, 1991.

Betachin. "Conflicts and Mediation between Couples." *Topics concerning the Families of Ethiopian Jews* 1 (1989).

———. "Topics in the Care of Families of a Different Cultural Background." *Topics concerning the Families of Ethiopian Jews* 4 (1990).

Doleve-Gandelman, Tsili. *Ethiopian Jews in Israel, Family Portraits: A Multi-Faceted View.* Jerusalem: Hebrew University of Jerusalem, 1989. (Hebrew).

Faitlovitch, Jacques. *Notes d'un voyage chez les Falachas (Juifs d'Abyssinie).* Paris, 1905.

Halévy, Joseph. "Travels in Abyssinia." in *Miscellany of Hebrew Literature,* ed. A. Lowy, tr. James Piciotto. London, 1877.

Kahana, Yael. *Among Long-Lost Brothers: A Young Israeli Woman Discovers the Falashas.* Tel Aviv: Am Oved, 1977. (In Hebrew).

Kaplan, Steven. *Les Falāshās.* Tournhout, Belgium: Brepols, 1990.

———. *The Beta Israel (Falasha) in Ethiopia: From Earliest Times to the Twentieth Century.* New York: New York University Press, 1992.

Kaplan, Steven, and Shoshana Ben-Dor. *Ethiopian Jews: An Annotated Bibliography.* Jerusalem: Ben Zvi Institute, 1988.

Leslau, Wolf. *Falasha Anthology.* New Haven: Yale University Press 1951; New York: Schocken, 1963, 1969.

Rosen, Chaim. "Questions and Answers on Ethiopian Jews." Jerusalem: Hadassah Women's Council, 1987.

————. "Advocacy and Dependency in the Ethiopian Community: A Case Study of Ashdod." Jerusalem: Ministry of Absorption, 1990.

Chaim, Rosen, and Daniel Chemtov. *Be 'Gobez' for the Sake of Your Health.* Jerusalem, 1992.

Schoenberger, Michelle. "The Falasha of Ethiopia: An Ethnographical Study." M.A. thesis, University of Cambridge, 1975.

Shelemay, Kay Kaufman. *Music, Ritual, and Falasha History.* East Lansing: Michigan State University Press, 1986.

Trevisan Semi, Emanuela. "The Beta Israel (Falasha): From Purity to Impurity," *Jewish Journal of Sociology* 25 (1987): 103–14.

Weil, Shalva. *Beliefs and Practices of Ethiopian Jews in Israel.* Jerusalem: Hebrew University of Israel, 1988, 1989. (Hebrew).

————. *Ethiopian One-Parent Families in Israel.* Jerusalem: Hebrew University of Jerusalem, 1991. (Hebrew).

Index